HOW POEMS
GET MADE

JAMES LONGENBACH

HOW POEMS
GET MADE

W. W. Norton & Company
INDEPENDENT PUBLISHERS SINCE 1923
NEW YORK • LONDON

For information about permission to reproduce selections from this book,
write to Permissions, W. W. Norton & Company, Inc., 500 Fifth Avenue,
New York, NY 10110

For information about special discounts for bulk purchases, please contact
W. W. Norton Special Sales at specialsales@wwnorton.com or 800-233-4830

Manufacturing by Quad Graphics Fairfield
Book design by Brooke Koven
Production manager: Julia Druskin

ISBN: 978-0-393-35520-8 (pbk.)

W. W. Norton & Company, Inc., 500 Fifth Avenue, New York, N.Y. 10110
www.wwnorton.com

W. W. Norton & Company Ltd., 15 Carlisle Street, London W1D 3BS

1 2 3 4 5 6 7 8 9 0

To Russ McDonald

CONTENTS

Preface   11

I.   Diction   15
II.   Syntax   27
III. Voice   37
IV.   Figure   49
V.   Rhythm   61
VI.   Echo   73
VII. Image   83
VIII. Repetition   95
IX.   Song   107
X.   Tone   119
XI.   Prose   131
XII. Poetry   141

Acknowledgments   153
Further Reading   155
Bibliography   161
Credits   169
Index   173

PREFACE

The impulse to be lyrical is driven by the need to feel unconstrained by ourselves. As poems have testified for centuries, we become lyrical when we suffer, when we love. But like poems themselves, we exist because of constraints—cultural and linguistic ways of organizing experience that allow us to know who we are. Why, when we're driven to be lyrical, are we gratified by the repetition of words, rhythms, and phrases? Why, having experienced the pleasure of a lyric poem once, do we want to experience it again? Why, when we're in love, can the repetition of an experience feel more fulfilling than the discovery?

This book describes how English-language poems get made from the most fundamental elements of their medium: the diction, syntax, figures, and rhythms of the English language itself. Because of a poet's organization of these elements, some poems may also be distinguished by qualities we call (more metaphorically) voice, image, or tone. These same qualities may distinguish prose, but through the simultaneous repetition and disruption of patterns, lyric poems aspire (sometimes literally, more often metaphorically) to the condition of song. Nobody rereads Keats's ode "To Autumn" to be reminded that in September leaves turn colors and fall from the trees; even if we know the poem by heart, we savor our experience of the poem's language as it unfolds in time, luring us forward.

There is of course a great deal to be said about diction, syntax, figuration, rhythm, or tone, and my goal is to offer succinct accounts of the poetic procedures with which any writer or reader would want to be intimate. Aspects of poems not registered in my chapter titles (such as line, rhyme, punctuation, disjunction) are treated along the way, each chapter building on the one preceding it, the whole book moving toward an ever-widening account of how poems are structured not as static vessels for meaning but as temporal events. While our first encounter with anything from a poem to a parking ticket might be revelatory, reading the same paragraph from a ticket as many times as one has read the ode "To Autumn" would probably not be satisfying—except if the paragraph's language enacts an emergence, a coming into being, that feels infinitely repeatable, richer over time.

Among the poets whose procedures I'll describe are Blake, Crane, Dickinson, Donne, Keats, Lawrence, Moore, Shakespeare, and Wyatt, along with a small array of contemporaries. Because they hold our attention as repeatable events, the best-known poems may seem wonderfully strange, especially after long acquaintance. And because their medium, the language we speak every day, is itself so familiar, we may experience the pleasure of what I'll call lyric knowledge—the eager rediscovery of what we already know—not only when we least expect it but when we expect it too well. A poem gets made not only in the act of composition but every time we read it again.

HOW POEMS
GET MADE

I

DICTION

The medium of Giorgione's "Tempest" is "oil on canvas"; the medium of Robert Rauschenberg's "Bed" is "oil and pencil on pillow, quilt, and sheet." Very few people handle oil paint as provocatively as Rauschenberg, but lots of people sleep on sheets. Those people may also draw a little, they may have a fine sense of color, but they respect the transaction between artist and medium that a particular work of art not only records but embodies. Sometimes, however, when the sheer otherness of the medium is foregrounded at the expense of a conventional signal of the artist's mind at work, people don't respect the transaction, in part because the artist doesn't covet such respect: how can art be something made of a bed sheet?

How can art be something made of words? Unlike the media most commonly associated with visual or musical artistry, words are harnessed by most people during almost every waking moment of their lives; they're more like sheets than like oil paint or the notes of the scale. Even small children are skilled manipulators of language, capable of detecting and repeating the most subtle nuances of tone. But children don't write the poems of Shakespeare or the novels of Henry James, and neither do most adults. We may sustain an easy mastery of language in our daily lives, but once we engage language as an artistic medium, that mastery is never secure: our relationship to language is constantly changing as we discover aspects of the medium that not only our prior failures but, more potently, our prior successes had occluded.

My medium is not language at large but the English language. When I was young I took this for granted, but over the years I've become increasingly conscious of the qualities shared by sentences because they're written in English, rather than German or French. The very word *medium*, derived from Latin, did not enter the English language until the Renaissance, when it referred to something that acts as an intermediary, like a piece of money or a messenger, and it was not until the nineteenth century that the word began to be used to describe the stuff from which art is made: the artistic medium enables a transaction between the artist and the world, and, over time, the history of those transactions has become inextricable from the medium itself. It's not coincidental that it was also in the nineteenth century that the word *medium* was first used to describe a person who conducts a séance, a person who exists simultaneously in the worlds of the living and the dead.

Every language has different registers of diction, but English comes by those registers in a particular way, one that reflects the entire history of the language. Old English, the language of the eighth- or ninth-century poem we call "The Seafarer," now looks and sounds to us like a foreign language, close to the German from which it was derived: with some study, one can see that the Old English line "bitre brēostceare gebiden hæbbe" means "bitter breast-cares abided have" or "I have abided bitter breast-cares." The language of Chaucer's fourteenth-century *Canterbury Tales*, or what we call Middle English, feels less strange, in part because its syntax now relies largely on word order rather than on word endings: "Thanne longen folk to goon on pilgrimages" or "then people long to go on pilgrimages." And the Modern English of the Renaissance we can read easily, because it is the language we speak today, even though the language has continued to evolve.

> Let me not to the marriage of true minds
> Admit impediments.

Many complicated factors determined this evolution, but one of the most important was the Norman invasion of England in 1066. Once Norman French became the language of the English court, a new vocabulary of words derived from Latin began to migrate into Germanic English. The Old English poet could abide *breast-cares*, but he could not go on a *pilgrimage* or suffer *impediments* or employ a *medium*; those Latinate words were not available to him. Even today, we raise *pigs* and *cows* (from German, via Old English) but eat *pork* and *beef* (from Latin, via French), because after the Norman conquest the peasants who raised animals generally spoke English while the noblemen who ate them spoke French. In the Renaissance, Latinate words were increasingly imported not only from French but directly from Latin itself, bequeathing to us an even wider menu of discriminations: *fear* (from German), *terror* (from French), *trepidation* (from Latin). English remains at its root a Germanic language, but around 70% of its vocabulary comes from non-English sources, and while the bulk of these borrowings had occurred by Shakespeare's lifetime, the language continues to expand, resulting in the variety of World Englishes spoken today.

Speakers of English may or may not be aware that their language is by its nature at odds with itself, but even the simplest deployment of English as an artistic medium depends on the juxtaposition of words with etymologically distant roots— words that sound almost as different from each other as do words from German and French. Chaucer's line "Thanne longen folk to goon on pilgrimages" mixes Germanic and Latinate diction strategically (the plain *folk* playing off the fancy *pilgrimages*), and Shakespeare's sentence "Let me not to the marriage of true minds / Admit impediments" does so more intricately, the Germanic monosyllables *let, true,* and *minds* consorting with the Latinate *marriage, admit,* and *impediments* to create the polyglot texture that speakers of English have come to recognize as the sound of eloquence itself. The extravagantly polyglot texture of Jean Toomer ("give virgin lips to cornfield concubines") or John Ashbery ("traditional surprise banquet of braised goat") feels idiosyncratic because it is also conventional, driven by the authors' intimacy with their expanding medium.

It's possible to suppress that texture, though not completely. In this passage from *Ulysses*, James Joyce writes as if Modern English were an almost exclusively Germanic language, giving priority to Germanic monosyllables and organizing the syntax as if English were still a highly inflected language, in which sense is less dependent on word order.

> Before born babe bliss had. Within womb won he
> worship.

And in this passage, Joyce writes English as if it were an almost exclusively Latinate language, frontloading Latinate vocabulary and weeding out as many Germanic words as possible.

> Universally that person's acumen is esteemed very little perceptive concerning whatsoever matters are being held as most profitably by mortals with sapience endowed.

But these feats of stylistic virtuosity sound more like the resuscitation of a dead language than the active deployment of a living one; it's difficult to speak English so single-mindedly. In contrast, Shakespeare's language feels fully alive in Sonnet 116, and yet its drama depends on the strategic juxtaposition of a Germanic phrase ("true minds") with a highly Latinate phrase that a speaker of English might never say ("admit impediments"), just as that speaker probably wouldn't say "babe bliss had" or "with sapience endowed." We don't speak of the cow who jumps over the moon as "translunar," though we could, and it is at such junctures that our language begins to function as an artistic medium: nothing is automatically a medium, though anything could be.

A medium, says the psychoanalyst Marian Milner in *On Not Being Able to Paint*, is a little bit of the world outside the self that, unlike the resolutely stubborn world at large, may be malleable, subject to the will while continuing to maintain its own character. The medium might be chalk, which cannot be made to produce the effects of watercolor. It might be a copperplate coated with a thin layer of silver and exposed to light. It might be a rosebush, pruned and fertilized into copious bloom, or an egg, exquisitely poached. In the realm of psychoanalysis, the medium is the analyst, a person who can be counted on to respond to the wishes of the analysand without needing to assert his own, as any person in an ordinary human relationship inevitably would.

But neither the analysand nor the artist may indulge in any infantile wish of dominating the medium completely. A visitor to Picasso's studio once recalled that, after squeezing out the paint on his palette, Picasso addressed it in Spanish, saying, "You are shit. You are nothing." Then he addressed the paint in French, saying, "You are beautiful. You are so fine." This conflict of attitudes (in this case so contentious that two languages are required to enact it) seems crucial. For if the artist loves the medium enough to submit himself to its actual qualities, resisting exaggerated notions of what the medium can do at his beck and call, then the result will likely be something recognizable as a work of art, a transaction between the mind and the world that is played out in the material reality of the medium.

The satisfaction of art may consequently be found in a poached egg or a child's drawing, but I suspect that we're most often moved to call a work of art great when we feel the full capacity of the medium at play, nothing suppressed, as if the artist's command of the medium and the long history of the medium's deployment by previous artists were coterminous—which, in a sense, they are.

> It is for Shakespeare's power of constitutive speech
> quite as if he had swum into our ken with it from
> another planet, gathering it up there, in its wealth,
> as something antecedent to the occasion and the
> need, and if possible quite in excess of them; some-
> thing that was to make of our poor world a great

flat table for receiving the glitter and clink of out-poured treasure.

While invoking Keats's sonnet "On First Looking into Chapman's Homer" ("Then felt I like some watcher of the skies / When a new planet swims into his ken"), this sentence by Henry James enacts the Shakespearean work it describes, overwhelming us with a feeling of unstoppable excess. The juxtaposition of Germanic bluntness and Latinate elaboration is immediately as apparent as it is in Shakespeare ("constitutive speech," "something antecedent," "occasion and the need," "quite in excess," "great flat table"), and, at the end of the sentence, as the last clause walks effortlessly to the finish line, the strategy is raised to virtuosic heights: "the glitter and clink of outpoured treasure."

This sentence sounds like James, but by performing the action it describes, the sentence also implies that linguistic virtuosity in Modern English is in some indelible way Shakespearean, and the implication, though easily abused, is not merely sentimental. Shakespeare was a powerful writer who in his lifetime was poised at exactly the right moment to take advantage of the medium that the English language had only recently become. He could reach for effects that had been unavailable to the poets of both "The Seafarer" and *The Canterbury Tales*, and because of the particular power with which he did so, poems we think of as great, poems that harness the full capacity of the medium, often tend to sound to us Shakespearean. But what we are really hearing in such poems is the medium at work; what we are hearing is the efforts of a great variety of writers to reach for the effects that Modern English most vigorously enables.

The Germanic and Latinate aspects of English are themselves

hardly monolithic, but English words derived from German may often seem vulgar or plain; English words derived from Latin may often seem officious or magical. Yet the particular way in which a lyric poem engineers the juxtaposition of such words may alter those associations instantly, if not permanently, making the bluntest monosyllables seem magical. The final sentence of Marianne Moore's "My Apish Cousins" (later called "The Monkeys") is an effortlessly Jamesian extravaganza spoken by a cat, who is enraged by people who make the experience of art seem unavailable to the simpler mammals.

> I shall never forget—that Gilgamesh among
> the hairy carnivora—that cat with the
>
> wedge-shaped, slate-gray marks on its forelegs and the
>   resolute tail,
> astringently remarking: "They have imposed on us with
>   their pale
>   half fledged protestations, trembling about
>   in inarticulate frenzy, saying
>   it is not for all of us to understand art, finding it
>   all so difficult, examining the thing
>
> as if it were something inconceivably arcanic, as
> symmetrically frigid as something carved out of chrysopras
>   or marble—strict with tension, malignant
>   in its power over us and deeper
>   than the sea when it proffers flattery in exchange
>   for hemp,
>   rye, flax, horses, platinum, timber and fur."

Until the final line, almost all the nouns in this sentence have been derived from Latin (*protestations, frenzy, tension, power, flattery, exchange*) and so have most of the modifiers (*inarticulate, difficult, inconceivably, symmetrically, frigid, malignant*). Of the verbs driving us through this exfoliation of dependent clauses, luring us through a verbal texture that is almost overwhelmingly rich but never grammatically unclear, about half of them are Latinate (*impose, examine, proffer*). When we are finally thrown into the list of nouns with which the sentence concludes, the mostly Germanic monosyllables seem to rise magically, extruded from the language preceding them: "hemp, / rye, flax, horses, platinum, timber and fur."

Moore's diction is not showy or contrived; she is acutely conscious of inherited gradations within the vocabulary we harness in every sentence we speak. So while the final sentence of "My Apish Cousins" is a theatrical manipulation of those gradations, it sounds not like a reduction of the medium ("babe bliss had") but like an inhabitation of the medium ("the glitter and clink of outpoured treasure"). After all, "My Apish Cousins" asks us to attend not to what is fancy or artificial but to what is fundamental and plain—*hemp, rye, flax*. And yet the poem also suggests that we recover our sense of wonder in the face of plain things only through highly intricate means. For while six of those final nouns could readily have been harnessed by the Old English poet of "The Seafarer" (*hemp, rye, flax, horses, timber, fur*), one of them stands out as egregiously Latinate: *platinum* was first discovered in the new world by the Spanish, who thought it was an inferior form of silver; they called it *platina*, a diminutive form of the word *plata*, meaning silver. Is platinum a false kind of silver or a thing unto itself, like hemp or flax?

It would be difficult to register the force of the collision of *proffers flattery* with *hemp, rye, flax* in a more exclusively Latinate language or a more exclusively Germanic language, but this does not mean that anything is lost when Moore's poem is translated into German or French; on the contrary, it means that something is discovered. We can't expect one language to replicate the effects to which another is particularly amenable, but the act of translation does, when the host language is engaged as a medium, create a new poem—a poem that asks us not simply to extract its meaning but to participate in the process of language becoming meaningful.

But what distinguishes that process in a great English poem is that often we feel we're grappling with more than one language at once, as if the act of writing in English were already an act of translation.

Death and life were not
Till man made up the whole,
Made lock, stock and barrel
Out of his bitter soul,
Aye, sun and moon and star, all,
And further add to that
That, being dead, we rise,
Dream and so create
Translunar Paradise.

The final line of this sentence from W. B. Yeats's "The Tower" could not be more different from the final line of "My Apish Cousins" ("rye, flax, horses"), but each poem makes its final line feel like a revelatory event. Working in the opposite direction from Moore, Yeats begins by restricting himself to words derived mostly from German (*dead, rise, dream*). Then a different language leaps from the page: "Translunar Paradise." To hear these two Latinate words in this sonic context is to feel the discovery of the spiritual realm Yeats is talking about, especially since the two Latinate words fill out the trimeter line ("Trans**lu**-nar **Par**adise") as elegantly as the Germanic monosyllables ("That, **being dead**, we **rise**").

The meaning of those two words is crucial to the poem, but if you translate the final lines from Latinate English into Germanic English (the word *paradise* means an enclosed garden, or what folks from around here call a *yard*), its effect is changed.

> That, being dead, we swoon,
> Dream and therefore make
> A yard beyond the moon.

Translate these lines into Latinate English, and the effect is also changed.

> That, being deceased, we levitate,
> Hallucinate and consequently create
> Translunar Paradise.

Because this diction is blandly consistent, the lines have nothing toward which to move, no feeling of discovery in which we may participate.

After brief acquaintance, we may remember a lyric poem's meaning more readily than the particularity of its medium; but our relationship with the poem grows richer to the degree that we're involved with the medium, seduced by the repeatable dis-covery of what we already know. The process of lyric knowledge captivates us beyond our knowledge of the poem's information as such, and if we're reading an English-language poem, this drama of discovery depends on our experience of one kind of diction resisting another, giving way to another. It also depends on our experience of English syntax.

II ✂

SYNTAX

Consider the anonymous lyric known as "Western Wind," which first appeared in a songbook probably owned by a musician in the court of Henry VIII. This is one of several ways you'll find the text printed today, its spelling and punctuation regularized.

> Western wind, when will you blow?
> The small rain down can rain.
> Christ, if my love were in my arms
> And I in my bed again.

This quatrain is cast in ballad measure, alternating tetrameter ("**Western wind**, when **will** you **blow**") and trimeter lines ("The **small** rain **down** can **rain**"), the two trimeters rhyming with each other ("rain" and "again"). The regularity of this form plays against the irregularity of the poem's syntax: a one-line question ("Western wind, when will you blow?") is followed by a one-line statement ("The small rain down can rain") and then

by a two-line exclamation ("Christ, if my love were in my arms /
And I in my bed again"), the syntax of this sentence for the first
time exceeding the duration of the line.

What happens if you arrange the lines of "Western Wind"
in a different order? The poem makes clear sense, but while
the form is identical (alternating tetrameter and trimeter lines
rhymed *xaxa*), the poem's structure is different.

> Christ, if my love were in my arms
> And I in my bed again.
> Western wind, when will you blow?
> The small rain down can rain.

Here, we turn from an experience of emotional longing to the
weather, an external drama that confirms the inner turmoil; the
feeling of confirmation is enforced by the two one-line sentences
with which the poem now concludes, a self-contained question
and a self-contained answer. Something happens in this shift
from interiority to exteriority, for we feel in both arenas the
power of absence, the desire for change, but something more
momentous happens in the original structure, in which our
expectations are not confirmed but shattered.

"Western Wind" begins by looking out, asking in the first
one-line sentence for the exterior world to change: "Western
wind, when will you blow?" The second one-line sentence makes
an observation about that world: "The small rain down can
rain." At this point, the poem is about nothing but weather—a
wish that the weather were different, a wish registered most poignantly in the phrase "small rain"; would that we were getting a
downpour, a deluge. Then the poem slaps us with new information, a revelation of erotic longing, reinforcing the slap with the

unexpected blasphemy ("Christ") and then, more potently, with a sentence that disrupts the established pattern of containment, the syntax suddenly refusing to be constrained by the line: "Christ, if my love were in my arms / And I in my bed again."

Different information would alter the poem, just as it would alter the sentence I examined from "The Tower."

> That, being dead, we rise,
> Dream and so create
> Translucent paragraphs.

But a rearrangement of the order in which we receive the information also alters the poem. Reading "Western Wind" line by line, sentence by sentence, we're made to feel not that we're receiving the results of an inquiry but that the inquiry is taking shape as the poem unfolds. The poem's greatest wish is to repeat the routine of daily life ("I in my bed again"), and the poem's structure makes the discovery of that wish feel permanently surprising. *Again*, as every child knows, is one of the most powerful words in the language.

"Did you ever read one of her Poems backward," asked Emily Dickinson of an unknown interlocutor about an unidentified poet, "because the plunge from the front overturned you? I sometimes (often have, many times) have—A something overtakes the Mind."

> The stalks are firmly rooted in ice.
> It is deep January. The sky is hard.
>
> The leaves hop, scraping on the ground,
> Like seeing fallen brightly away.

Snow sparkling like eyesight falling to earth
Is merely the moving of a tongue.

They have heads in which a captive cry
Without legs or, for that, without heads,

Has arms without hands. They have trunks
In this bleak air, the broken stalks.

Bad is final in this light.
The field is frozen. The leaves are dry,

As absent as if we were asleep.
He is not here, the old sun.

What you have just read is the beginning of Wallace Stevens's "No Possum, No Sop, No Taters," a poem about the deprivations of wartime rationing in the early 1940s, except that you have read it backwards, concluding with the poem's first line. Though the original ordering of this passage contains the same number of sentences arranged in the same number of unrhymed couplets, I have altered the punctuation, recombining the constituent pieces of the poem's syntax into new grammatical shapes. In doing so, I have needed to alter just two words (*sparkles* to *sparkling* and *have* to *has*).

But while the resulting syntax is coherent, the *something* produced by reading "No Possum, No Sop, No Taters" backwards is different from the *something* produced by what Dickinson called the plunge from the front. To conclude the poem with the act of personifying the sun ("He is not here") makes that figure, though it records an absence, feel like a brazened wish to find human companionship in the starkly inhuman natural world.

>The field is frozen. The leaves are dry,
>
>As absent as if we were asleep.
>He is not here, the old sun.

To begin with the personification makes it feel like a passingly familiar metaphor, hardly worth noticing.

>He is not here, the old sun,
>As absent as if we were asleep.
>
>The field is frozen. The leaves are dry.

Why are these sentences so amenable to rearrangement?

The nature of English syntax is determined by many factors, but just as we may observe a great deal about a poem's diction merely by focusing on the arrangement of different kinds of words, so may we observe a great deal simply by comparing the way in which sentences arrange their constituent phrases and clauses. Throughout "No Possum, No Sop, No Taters," Stevens's syntax is predominantly paratactic: his clauses, each with its own subject and verb, are arranged side by side, without any sense of hierarchy (*para*, from the Greek, means *beside*): "It is deep January. The sky is hard." While clauses may be linked by coordinating conjunctions in paratactic syntax (*It is deep January, and the sky is hard*), Stevens lets his clauses stand alone, making the poem sound ceremoniously hieratic.

The sentence *Because it is deep January, the sky is hard* is in contrast hypotactic: because the two clauses are linked by a subordinating conjunction, one clause depends on the other (*hypo*, from the Greek, means *under*). We tend to employ hypotactic syntax when describing the hierarchical relationship between causes and effects in a narrative or between facts and conclusions in an argument, and throughout "No Possum, No Sop, No Taters," Stevens isn't doing either of those things; his mostly paratactic syntax builds a structure through association and juxtaposition. Charged information is accumulating, but because we don't yet know why, the poem sounds not only hieratic but ominous.

Given this reliance on parataxis, "No Possum, No Sop, No Taters" is much more amenable to rearrangement than a poem featuring hypotactic syntax.

> In the darkest evening of the year,
> Between the woods and frozen lake,
> To stop without a farmhouse near—
> My little horse must think it queer
>
> To watch his woods fill up with snow.
> He will not see me stopping here;
> His house is in the village though.
> Whose woods these are I think I know.

Robert Frost is telling a story; Stevens is not. The syntax of "No Possum, No Sop, No Taters" avoids causal relationships between its clauses, allowing the poem to make plausible sense both backwards and forwards: "*The leaves hop, scraping on the ground. It is deep January. The sky is hard. The stalks are firmly rooted in ice*" or "*The stalks are firmly rooted in ice. The sky is*

hard. *It is deep January. The leaves hop, scraping on the ground.*"
It matters in Frost's "Stopping by Woods on a Snowy Evening,"
in contrast, whether it is a horse or a person who watches his
woods fill up with snow.

But less obviously, it also matters whether we move from the
behavior of leaves to a more general sense of the month of January, or whether we move from a sense of January to the behavior
of leaves; it matters in "Western Wind" whether we move from
weather to erotic longing or from erotic longing to weather.
The fact that a predominantly paratactic syntax enables a lyric's
rearrangement does not undermine the lyric's plunge from the
front; it alerts us to the inevitability of the plunge, one thing
following another for a purpose that reveals itself in the time it
takes to read the poem.

Consider the first stanza, which is also the first sentence, of
John Donne's "The Canonization."

> For God's sake hold your tongue, and let me love,
>   Or chide my palsy, or my gout,
> My five grey hairs, or ruined fortune flout,
>   With wealth your state, your mind with arts improve,
>   Take you a course, get you a place,
>   Observe his honour, or his grace,
> Or the King's real, or his stamped face
>   Contemplate, what you will, approve,
>   So you will let me love.

This sentence contains eleven independent clauses, and until
the stanza's final line, they are arranged without any subordination: *hold your tongue, let me love, chide my palsy, flout my
fortune, improve your state, take a course, get a place, observe his*

grace, contemplate his face, approve what you will. Formally, the stanza's meter and rhyme scheme put pressure on this paratactic accumulation of imperatives: beginning with a quatrain rhymed *abba*, the stanza moves to a more tightly rhymed tetrameter couplet ("Take you a course, get you a place, / Observe his honor, or his grace") that quickens the act of listing and makes the entire sentence feel as if it were tumbling forward, bearing down on its final line with an inexhaustible reserve of syntactical repetition.

Then, in the stanza's final line, the syntax changes. We encounter the poem's first subordinate clause (*so that you will let me love*), and this shift to hypotaxis enacts the poem's argument: after being told many times over what to do, we're told why. Were the stanza to begin with hypotaxis, moving backwards, the accumulation of parallel clauses would feel like a static confirmation of what we know, rather than a strategically pressurized suspension through which the poem's purpose is revealed.

Once having been found, however, the purpose needs to get lost. The second stanza of "The Canonization" shifts its syntactical energies, moving from the first stanza's single imperative to a sequence of one-line interrogatives.

> Alas, alas, who's injur'd by my love?
>> What merchant's ships have my sighs drowned?
> Who says my tears have overflowed his ground?
>> When did my colds a forward spring remove?

Throughout the poem, these shifts between sentences that alternately confirm or conflict with the lineation, between sentences turning abruptly from one mode or tense to another, make us feel that the poem progresses by a succession of spontaneous choices, as if the poem's structure were not premeditated but were happening in real time. As a result, when the second stanza shifts from these one-liners to a longer hypotactic sentence, reasserting the poem's argument—

> Soldiers find wars, and lawyers find out still
>   Litigious men, which quarrels move,
>   Though she and I do love

—the reassertion feels again a discovery, a source of pleasure even after the poem's argument is grasped.

Given Donne's sporadic embrace of parataxis, certain of his stanzas will read as elegantly backwards as they do forwards, the form (driven by the stanza's meter and rhyme) unchanged but the structure (driven by the syntax coursing through the stanza) different. Revealing as such rearrangements may be, however, they sacrifice Donne's crucially delayed shifts from parataxis to hypotaxis, shifts that make Donne's conclusions seem simultaneously inevitable and unprecedented. Just as the drama of Yeats's "The Tower" depends on a movement from one kind of diction to another, the forward plunge of "The Canonization" depends not simply on what kinds of sentences the poem contains but on the order in which those sentences appear, one kind of syntax giving way to another. As Coleridge famously proposed, poetry is "the best words" (diction) in "the best order" (syntax).

A poet writes sentences; the sentences appear in the order in which he writes them. How might a poem's most inevitable plunge be found? Paradoxically, John Koethe actually wrote his 207-line poem "The Constructor" backwards, moving from its final sentence—

Why do I feel so happy?

—to its penultimate sentence—

How could this quiet feeling

Actually exist?

—and so on, until he wrote finally what became the first sentence of the poem: "They strike me less as actual persons than as abstract / Ghosts of an idea." The poem might have been perpetuated in the order in which Koethe actually wrote its sentences, but one can sense immediately the attraction of moving backwards: what was originally a governing thesis, a question to be explored ("Why do I feel so happy?"), becomes in the reordering not a stolid given but an unforeseen gift. The simple flatness of the question feels in the final position uncanny, driven into existence by unforeseen forces, just as on a much smaller scale the final two-line sentence of "Western Wind" does.

One might say that my strategic rewriting of Frost ("My little horse must think it queer / To watch his woods fill up with snow") is similarly transformative; it sounds a little like John Ashbery, whose elegantly hypotactic sentences provide a syntax of cause and effect while at the same time refusing to provide us with a plausible narrative of cause and effect. But my point is not that syntactical procedures need to be manhandled in order to be interesting. My point is that lyric poems enact infinitely repeatable dramas of surprise through their syntax and that, even more fundamentally, English syntax and diction are themselves surprising. Poetry happens, as Shakespeare puts it, in the "telling" of what is already "told."

III ✵

VOICE

Let's say you want to write a poem that by its fourth or fifth syllable sounds urgently spoken, a poem that makes its readers feel almost instantly engaged with an interlocutor, perhaps even making them feel late to the party—that the conversation is well underway. You might begin with an imperative that fills out a single pentameter line, the majority of its syllables ringing changes on a single vowel (*God, hold, tongue, love*) so that the line feels trippingly spontaneous and yet so tersely epigrammatic that it forestalls argument.

> For God's sake hold your tongue, and let me love.

Or you might offer a charged exclamation, an even punchier string of monosyllables overriding the iambic rhythm, the majority of those syllables sharing no consonant with another (*he, stark, mad*) so that the mouth is forced to reshape itself with every syllable, the resulting utterance feeling deliberately considered.

He is stark mad.

Or you might ask a question, an aggressive enjambment divid-
ing subject from predicate and throwing extra pressure on the
syllable (the first-person pronoun) with which the line both
begins and ends, this elegantly balanced sonic decorum tem-
pering the line's narcissism while also displaying it.

> I wonder by my troth, what thou and I
> Did, till we loved?

No English-language poet is more thrillingly efficient than
John Donne at establishing the illusion of a speaking voice.
Shakespeare's blank verse often generates the illusion as well, but
it was Donne's achievement to have harnessed such dramatic
energy within the compass of the lyric poem, and one feels the
lasting influence of Donne's strategies in the opening lines of
poets as different from one another as Robert Browning—

> But do not let us quarrel any more.

—Marianne Moore—

> Why so desolate?

—and D. H. Lawrence.

> You tell me I am wrong.

These strategies continue to be crucial for poets writing today,
poets as different from one another as Frank Bidart—

What should I have done?

—John Ashbery—

Time, you old miscreant!

—and Ellen Bryant Voigt.

I made a large mistake I left my house

When we say that a poem presents us with a strong sense of voice, what we're often in fact saying is that the poem sounds like Donne. We're employing a metaphor, the *speaker* of the poem, which describes not how poems are destined to sound but how we've become accustomed to particular ways of organizing the medium of the English language into particular sonic patterns. Asking someone to write a sentence with a strong voice is like asking a chef to prepare a dish that tastes good. If she's successful, that chef will be thinking about particular ingredients; syntax and diction are readily at hand, but you can't reach into the pantry for a cup of voice.

It's nonetheless seductive to imagine ourselves as intimate listeners, rather than more distant readers; Socrates would have approved of this prejudice, which is nearly as old as western culture itself. But our impulse to employ the metaphor of a speaking voice has more recently been conditioned by the lingering power of the New Criticism, the literary critical movement that, while it flourished from the 1930s through the 1960s, encouraged several generations of readers to distinguish between the author and the speaker of a poem—often by foregrounding the example of Donne.

"Every poem," said Cleanth Brooks and Robert Penn Warren in the first edition of their influential anthology, *Understanding Poetry*, published in 1938, "implies a speaker of the poem." In part, Brooks and Warren were providing readers with a way of coming to terms with the unfamiliar difficulties of certain modernist poems; it's initially helpful to think of the disjunctive verbal texture of T. S. Eliot's "Love Song of J. Alfred Prufrock" as an utterance spoken by a particular person. But in later editions of *Understanding Poetry*, expediency hardens into method: "always when we are making acquaintance with a poem," urged Brooks and Warren, "we must answer these questions: (1) Who is speaking? (2) Why?" These questions ask us to forget that the *speaker* of the poem is a metaphor; they ask us to define poems as utterances driven by the presence of a speaking subject (which poems may or may not seem to be), rather than strategic deployments of various kinds of syntax and diction (which poems always are).

The Eliot of "Prufrock" and *The Waste Land* was a poet who, like so many others, had learned from Donne how to establish the illusion of a speaking presence in just a few syllables: "Let us go then, you and I"; "My nerves are bad to-night. Yes, bad." To borrow the influential language Eliot used to describe Donne's poems, Eliot's poems up to *The Waste Land* are poems of "psychology," poems that dramatize states of mind "composed of odds and ends in constant flux and manipulated by desire and fear."

Remarks like these helped to establish Donne's central place in the New Criticism, but Eliot never set out merely to change taste; he set out to write the best poems he could muster, and as his own aesthetic goals changed, his relationship to Donne changed. In the years following the publication of *The Waste*

Land in 1922, as Eliot accumulated the fragments he would eventually bring together to make *The Hollow Men* three years later, a different kind of poem began to emerge—a poem that does not encourage us to feel that it is spoken by a discrete human subject with a particular psychology. While the poem feels anguished, it is not self-dramatizing, like "Prufrock"; the utterance feels oracular, dislocated, as if it were emerging not from within but from beyond human experience.

> The eyes are not here
> There are no eyes here

The author of these lines has no more use for Donne; he has even less use for the poet of "Prufrock." While no poem is actually spoken on the page, these lines don't deploy Donne's strategies for creating the illusion of spokenness. They encourage us to pay attention not to the perceiving sensibility we might imagine behind the poem but to the world that exists independent of that sensibility.

Such suspicion of psychology, a suspicion not only of the narrow space of the mind but of the lyric's investment in the illusion of that space, is not in the twentieth century unique to the later Eliot. One feels it in poets of certain strains of the American avant-garde, poets from Louis Zukofsky writing in response to the early Eliot to Susan Howe writing today; the variety of poets who became associated with the magazine *L=A=N=G=U=A=G=E* were more or less united by their desire to write poems that could not be imagined as being spoken, poems that could not be accounted for by New Critical methods of reading. While Eliot's swerve away from Donne was driven in part by the Christianity he embraced publicly in

1927, the rejection of the possibly pernicious illusion of the self-determining human subject was driven in these poets by the conjunction of Marxism and post-structuralism.

Donne has survived these debates, just as he survived the censure of Pope and Johnson in the eighteenth century, when a preference for classical balance and poise made Donne's syntactical performances seem garish. But the value of these debates is that they don't allow us to take for granted the kind of work Donne accomplished; that is, we're made to consider the precise linguistic mechanisms through which the illusion of a poem's speaker is constructed, rather than assuming that poems always have speakers, the way people have tongues. How did Donne do it? How, after the shock of his opening lines, did he keep doing it for the duration of the whole poem?

Think back to my discussions of diction and syntax. It may seem that a sentence dominated by highly Latinate diction will tend to sound written, while a sentence dominated by Germanic monosyllables will tend to sound spoken; similarly, it may seem that elaborately hypotactic syntax will sound written, while simpler syntactical constructions sound spoken. But in fact a poem's sentences will feel increasingly dramatic to the degree that we're made to attend to the pattern of their syllables unfolding in time; and more precisely constituent of a poem's degree of spokenness than any particular kind of diction or syntax is the strategic interplay between different kinds of diction and syntax. Especially as this interplay is itself played out over a poem's lineation, the resulting utterance may feel extruded from the poem's emerging occasion, as if the voice or self we presume to be driving the utterance were not given but emergent.

We've seen that the first stanza of "The Canonization" consists of one sentence, an imperative dominated by parataxis ("For
God's sake hold your tongue, and let me love") until its final line
("So you will let me love"). The sixty-seven words in this sentence are overwhelmingly monosyllabic; only eight of the words
have more than one syllable, and while Latinate words abound
(*state, arts, course, place, grace, real, face*), they are easily absorbed
by the exclusively Germanic diction with which the sentence
both begins ("For God's sake hold your tongue") and ends ("let
me love"). Syntactically, the final line's shift to subordination is
delayed by a long list of simple imperatives (*hold your tongue, let
me love, child my palsy*, and so on).

This syntactical shifting continues throughout the poem's
subsequent stanzas, and when we reach its conclusion, a poem
that began by frontloading plain diction and paratactic syntax
becomes a hypotactic extravaganza littered with egregiously
Latinate vocabulary (*invoke, reverend, hermitage*).

> And by these hymns, all shall approve
>   Us canonized for love.
>
>
> And thus invoke us: "you whom reverend love
>   Made one another's hermitage,
> You, to whom love was peace, that now is rage,
>   Who did the whole world's soul contract, and drove
>   Into the glasses of your eyes
>   So made such mirrors, and such spies,
> That they did all to you epitomize,
>   Countries, towns, courts, beg from above
>   A pattern of your love."

What has happened here? "The Canonization" begins by commanding the listener to stop talking ("hold your tongue"), but it concludes by transforming its listener into a speaker, who is enjoined to address the poem's lovers in the second person ("you whom reverend love"). In this final sentence, the listener speaks in the imperative, but the main verb is delayed by a sequence of parallel modifying clauses for so long ("whom reverend love / Made one another's hermitage"—"to whom love was peace"— "who did the whole world's soul contract"—"who drove / Into the glasses of your eyes . . . Countries, towns, courts") that when the verb finally appears ("beg"), it feels so syntactically satisfying that the poem's forever startling conclusion feels irrefutable: the poem's haughty speaker has been humbled, enjoined to beg—to "beg from above." Who could have heard it coming?

This kind of conflict between what feel like different voices, explicit in "The Canonization," is implicit in any poem that invites us to participate in the dramatized illusion of spokenness.

> You tell me I am wrong.
> Who are you, who is anybody to tell me I am wrong?
> I am not wrong.
>
> In Syracuse, rock left bare by the viciousness of Greek women,
> No doubt you have forgotten the pomegranate trees in flower,
> Oh so red, and such a lot of them.

The diction of these opening lines of D. H. Lawrence's "Pomegranate" is colloquial, the syntax untroubled by enjambment. But what matters most is that, like Donne, Lawrence enacts shifts in diction and syntax that make the poem feel produced

instantly on the page. While the first stanza features hypotactic syntax ("who is anybody to tell me I am"), the syntax of
the second stanza avoids subordination, its noun phrases hov-
ering in placid reverie ("rock left bare"—"viciousness of Greek
women"—"pomegranate trees in flower"). Then the violence of
hypotaxis intrudes.

> Do you mean to tell me you will see no fissure?

And then the reverie revives itself.

> The end cracks open with the beginning:
> Rosy, tender, glittering within the fissure.

But not for long.

> Do you mean to tell me there should be no fissure?
> No glittering, compact drops of dawn?
> Do you mean it is wrong, the gold-filmed skin, integument,
>   shown ruptured?

It's almost tempting to say that, speaking metaphorically,
"Pomegranate" is a dialogue between two voices, but what the
poem's procedures more precisely suggest is that we're inclined
to reach for the metaphor of voice not when we hear one consistent utterance but when we feel different kinds of diction,
syntax, and lineation working against one another: something happens in our act of reading the poem, something gets
made. "I prefer my heart to be broken. / It is so lovely, dawn-
kaleidoscopic within the crack," admits Lawrence in the poem's

final stanza, reverie eclipsing confrontation but also justifying its presence in a poem that is itself strategically broken, willfully at odds with itself.

Brokenness in no way implies a dearth of rigor or an acquiescence to chance.

> another heavy frost what doesn't die or fly away
> the groundhog for instance the bear is deep in sleep I'm
>   thinking
> a lot about sleep translation I'm not sleeping much
> who used to be a champion of sleep
> ex-champions are pathetic my inner parent says the world
> is full of evil death cruelty degradation not sleeping
> scores only 2 out of 10
>   but a moral sense
> is exhausting I am exhausted a coma looks good to me
> if only I could be sure there'd still be dreams it's what I miss
>   the most
> even in terrible dreams at least you feel what you feel not what
> you're supposed to feel your house burns down so what
> if you survived you rake the ashes sobbing

In contrast to Lawrence's "Pomegranate," in which most of the lines are end-stopped and syntactically complete, almost all the lines of Ellen Bryant Voigt's "Sleep" are enjambed, the lines refusing to allow us to process a completed syntactical phrase or clause without interruption. A clause may appear within a line ("the bear is deep in sleep"; "I am exhausted"), but the poem's eschewal of punctuation makes it difficult for us to rest within the completed clause. The formal pressure of line does not clar-

ify the structural work of syntax, as it might even without the
assistance of punctuation—

> But a moral sense is exhausting
> I am exhausted
> A coma looks good to me

—but instead forces us to inhabit the onslaught of syntax more
precisely as what it is: a rapid concatenation of multiple syntactical patterns carrying multiple tones and, as a result, fos-
tering the illusion of a human being speaking from within the
moment of discovering what she is driven to say.

The poem sounds like what we imagine spontaneity to be,
but the relinquishment of punctuation no more contributes
to freedom from structural and formal restraint than does the
relinquishment of meter. The degree to which Voigt's poem
sounds urgently spoken depends on the same procedures as
Lawrence or Donne—

> you tell me I am wrong who are you who is
> anybody to tell me I am wrong I am not wrong

—except that in "Sleep" the torqueing energy of the syntactical
shifts has become impossible to ignore.

What is the wish for a poem to have a voice a wish for? At
best, it is a wish for visceral immediacy, a wish that poems by
Donne, Lawrence, and Voigt repay handsomely. But at worst,
it is a wish for the certainty of human presence, rather than the
fluctuating work of language—a wish for reliable information
rather than the inexhaustible pleasure of lyric knowledge. It may

be useful to differentiate the historical *author* from the fictional *speaker* of the poem, but it's also instructive to remember that the Latinate word *immediacy* means *without the intervention of a medium*: a poem is nothing without its medium. Because of the disposition of its language, one poem may feel spoken while another may not, but all poems are scrupulously made, forged from the syntax, diction, and figuration at hand.

IV ❧

FIGURE

"The greatest thing by far is to have a command of metaphor," proclaimed Aristotle. What might he have meant?

> For God's sake hold your tongue, and let me love,
>   Or chide my palsy, or my gout,
> My five grey hairs, or ruined fortune flout,
>   With wealth your state, your mind with arts improve.

Unlike a metonymy, which conflates two logically related things, a metaphor merges two unrelated things: in Donne's lines, one can no more *chide* a palsy or *hold* one's tongue than one can *fall* asleep (a spatial metaphor suggesting that human consciousness exists above unconsciousness) or *spend* one's time (a mercantile metaphor suggesting that time is a commodity). As George Lakoff and Mark Johnson point out in *Metaphors We Live By*, the power of these conventional metaphors is enormous: "he *sank* into a coma"—"*budget* your time." Such figures distinguish not only poems but almost every sentence we utter; everyone is a master of metaphor. Yet often we remain unaware of a metaphor's implications—until a poem asks us to become aware.

We've seen that a poem's characteristic plunge from the front depends on its movement between different levels of diction or between different kinds of syntax; similarly, the way in which a poem orders its metaphors, asking us to inhabit their relationships over time, is more powerful than any particular metaphor, judged in isolation.

> For a Tear is an Intellectual thing
> And a Sigh is the Sword of an Angel King
> And the bitter groan of the Martyrs woe
> Is an Arrow from the Almighties bow.

This quatrain from William Blake's "The Grey Monk" contains three prominent metaphors: *a tear is an intellectual thing, a sigh is a sword, a groan is an arrow*. Though the figures are far from conventional (we don't say that a *sigh* is a *sword* in the easy way in which we say that we *fall* asleep), the paratactic syntax makes the movement from one figure to the next feel rationally considered: *a tear is . . . and a sigh is . . . and a groan is*. In addition, the second two figures are not only syntactically but conceptually parallel: an inarticulate mode of human expression (a *sigh* or a *groan*) is in each case compared to a means of physical violence (a *sword* or an *arrow*), and the repeated logic makes the extravagance of the figures seem more reassuringly predictable (*a sigh is the sword . . . and the bitter groan . . . is an arrow*).

Here is another way in which a poem might order its metaphors.

Figure [51]

And wrecks passed without sound of bells,
The calyx of death's bounty giving back
A scattered chapter, livid hieroglyph,
The portent wound in corridors of shells.

Unlike Blake's metaphors, the metaphors in this quatrain from Hart Crane's "At Melville's Tomb" do not reinforce one another, building a sense of parallel significance; instead, they extend one another, pushed by the quatrain's initially right-branching syntax into increasingly unexpected realms of significance: *wrecks passed, the resulting calyx giving back a hieroglyph which was in turn a portent.* When the young Crane submitted this poem to *Poetry* magazine in 1926, Harriet Monroe queried him about this logic: "You ask me how a *portent* can possibly be wound in a *shell*," responded the exasperated but determinedly polite Crane, "I ask you how Blake could possible say that 'a *sigh* is a *sword* of an Angel King.'" But while Crane could argue that Blake's metaphors are as unconventional as his own, and while Crane's metaphor feels explicable in itself, the relationship of this figure to the figures preceding it feels equivocal, possibly discordant.

What Crane called his poem's "logic of metaphor" is by no means haphazard, however.

And wrecks passed without sound of bells . . .

The ship sinks without ceremony, no bells, producing a whirlpool that sucks its sailors and cargo down to death. But once the ship disappears, the whirlpool becomes a cornucopia that delivers a bounty of wreckage to the surface.

> The calyx of death's bounty giving back
> A scattered chapter, livid hieroglyph . . .

This bounty (the broken and reconfigured pieces of the ship) is now legible only as an incomplete story, a scattered chapter, or as a collection of inexplicable signs, hieroglyphs. The scattered chapter is like a hieroglyph, which is like

> The portent wound in corridors of shells.

"About as much definite knowledge might come from all this as anyone might gain from the roar of his own veins, which is easily heard (haven't you ever done it?) by holding a shell close to one's ear," Crane told Monroe, explicating the final leap from the figure of the hieroglyph to the inexplicable portent one hears within the calyx of a shell. Crane was eager to suggest that each of his figures is grounded in ordinary experience, but what makes the figuration nonetheless difficult to process is the variety of unprecedented realms of experience (shipwreck, harvest, story-telling, crustaceans) toward which the syntax pushes us. The effect of the poem is due not so much to the extravagance of its metaphors as to their order—to the way in which the poem's syntax moves forward in an act of discovery, not an act of confirmation.

"At Melville's Tomb" is a highly idiosyncratic poem, but the serial organization of its figures is in fact central to English-language poetry in a way that Blake's sequence of parallel figures is not. "Generally they are ill constructed," said the influential New Critic John Crowe Ransom of Shakespeare's sonnets: like Harriet Monroe reading Crane, he was perplexed by the rapid and surprising way in which Shakespeare's metaphors supersede

Figure [53]

one another, phrase by phrase, line by line. But Ransom was not responding to an intriguing poem by an unknown poet; he was objecting to an aspect of Shakespeare's verse that had long provoked admiration and wonder. Writing about the sonnets more than a century earlier, John Keats found their figuration thrilling.

> I never found so many beauties in the sonnets—they
> seem to be full of fine things said unintentionally—
> in the intensity of working out conceits—Is this to
> be borne?

The illusion of spontaneity ("things said unintentionally") generated by the quixotic unfolding of figurative language ("the working out of conceits") was what Keats admired most about the sonnets, and he went on to quote the second quatrain of the twelfth sonnet as an example of an achievement so astonishing it could hardly be borne.

Here is the entire poem.

> When I do count the clock that tells the time,
> And see the brave day sunk in hideous night,
> When I behold the violet past prime
> And sable curls all silvered o'er with white,
> When lofty trees I see barren of leaves,
> Which erst from heat did canopy the herd,
> And summer's green all girded up in sheaves
> Borne on the bier with white and bristly beard;
> Then of thy beauty do I question make
> That thou among the wastes of time must go,
> Since sweets and beauties do themselves forsake,

And die as fast as they see others grow,
And nothing 'gainst time's scythe can make defence
Save breed to brave him when he takes thee hence.

The formal expectations aroused by the typically Shakespearean rhyme scheme (*abab cdcd efef gg*) suggest that this sonnet
breaks into three four-line units followed by a two-line unit. But
the structural expectations aroused by the sonnet's hypotactic
syntax suggest that its single sentence breaks into an eight-line
unit (three parallel adverbial clauses of irregular length—
"When I do count"—"When I behold"—"When lofty trees I
see"), followed by a four-line unit inaugurated by the sentence's
independent clause ("Then of thy beauty do I question make"),
followed by a two-line unit inaugurated by a second independent clause ("And nothing . . . can make defence"). The sonnet's
formal arrangement stands at odds with its structure, and the
figuration reinforces the dynamic work of the syntax, not the
static paradigm of the rhyme scheme.

The first of the sonnet's three adverbial clauses offers conventional metaphors, the kind we use in most any sentence we
utter: the clock *tells* the time, day is *sunk* in night. In the second
adverbial clause, the metaphors become more extravagant; the
violet is *past prime*, the sable curls are *silvered*. And while it's not
difficult to link these metaphors of physical decay to the earlier metaphors for temporal change, the metaphors in the third
and longest adverbial clause—the lines that provoked Keats's
wonder—become increasingly difficult to track.

When lofty trees I see barren of leaves,
Which erst from heat did canopy the herd,

Figure   [55]

And summer's green all girded up in sheaves
Borne on the bier with white and bristly beard . . .

While the barren trees function, like the violets and sable
curls, as figures for change, the additional figure treating the
once-green trees as solicitous shepherds ("did *canopy* the herd")
throws us into more unpredictable arenas of significance, as
does the figure personifying the now faded sheaves as the dead
body ("Borne on the bier") of an elderly man ("white and bristly
beard"). What's more, the figures seem to generate one another
as much by vagaries of sound as by the logic of sense, the syllable
bier extending into *beard*. "Is this to be borne?" asked Keats at
this point, echoing the poem itself: three dependent clauses are
bearing down with increasingly extravagant figuration on the
emergent independent clause, whose language seems suddenly
transparent: "Then of thy beauty do I question make."

The remainder of the sonnet's sentence is less densely fig-
ured but increasingly wayward. For while many of the earlier
metaphors emphasize natural change (violets, curls, trees),
beauty now seems in charge of his own destiny, able to choose
between saving himself and forsaking himself to death: "beau-
ties do themselves forsake, / And die as fast as they see others
grow." But how could a violet choose not to fade? How could
a man with bristly beard not end up borne on a bier? Then,
in the couplet, an egregiously conventional metaphor ("time's
scythe") suggests that beauty's life is not naturally but violently
terminated. But even if old men's beards will never turn sable
again, deciduous trees do regain their leaves; perennial violets
do return with spring. The final couplet offers the sound of
epigrammatic closure, as final couplets almost inevitably do,

but the order of the sonnet's metaphors remains provocatively linear, each one suggested by but not necessarily at peace with the figures preceding it.

Shakespeare's sonnets may be the most influential body of lyric poems in the language—which has little to do with the fact that they happen to be sonnets; it has to do with their intricate collusions of figuration and syntax. Keats's judgment sharpens our sense of the particular nature of their influence; Ransom's judgment makes it more difficult for us to take the particular nature of their influence for granted: the sonnets will seem ill-constructed only if we imagine structure to be a grid-like pattern imposed on language, rather than a dynamic event that happens in the incremental act of reading sentences. A metaphor is not a static vessel for meaning.

Consider the first three lines of Keats's "Ode to a Nightingale": the poet's heart aches, we don't yet know why, but his senses are numb, reminding us that the ache is not physical; he feels as if he had dosed himself with opiates, as did other romantic writers such as Coleridge and De Quincey.

> My heart aches, and a drowsy numbness pains
>> My sense, as though of hemlock I had drunk,
> Or emptied some dull opiate to the drains.

"More than a figure of speech," says Keats's most recent biographer, "Keats's 'dull opiate emptied to the drains' frankly admits his own laudanum habit." But how can we know that the lines are more than figurative? Why employ a mathematical figure ("more than") implying that figuration itself is inadequate or incomplete?

"We need to cure ourselves of the wish for biography," says

Figure [57]

the psychoanalyst Adam Phillips, suggesting that the stories we tell about our lives, inasmuch as they fix our lives, cannot be driven other than by anxiety and fear. And if biographies of poets were written in the manner of lyric poems, we'd find them wayward and inefficient, possibly maddening—which might be, from the psychoanalytic perspective, a good thing. Treated as a vessel for meaning, Keats's figure ("dull opiates") becomes the proof for the speculation it also provokes, the wish for biographical knowledge transforming the repeatable pleasure of lyric knowledge into a condition that needs to be cured. But in any case, as the "Ode to a Nightingale" continues, Keats rejects both opiates and alcohol, declaring that he will leave the world where "youth grows pale, and spectre-thin" on the "viewless wings of Poesy." Like Shakespeare's and Crane's, Keats's figuration is constantly shifting, generating new meanings so quickly that its author seems barely able to keep up with his own invention.

Yet the force of Keats's metaphors is, however equivocal, not inconsequential: when he wrote this sonnet (inscribed on a blank page in his copy of Shakespeare's poems), he knew he was dying.

> Bright star, would I were steadfast as thou art—
>   Not in lone splendor hung aloft the night,
> And watching, with eternal lids apart,
>   Like nature's patient, sleepless eremite,
> The moving waters at their priestlike task
>   Of pure ablution round earth's human shores,
> Or gazing on the new soft-fallen mask
>   Of snow upon the mountains and the moors;
> No—yet still steadfast, still unchangeable,
>   Pillow'd upon my fair love's ripening breast,

To feel for ever its soft swell and fall,
    Awake for ever in a sweet unrest,
Still, still to hear her tender-taken breath,
And so live ever—or else swoon to death.

Although this sonnet begins by declaring a wish for metaphorical equivalence ("would I were steadfast as thou art"), it spends its first two quatrains objecting to the implications of the metaphor, producing new figures in the process: Keats would be as steadfast as the star but not inasmuch as the star is in turn like a sleepless hermit watching the movement of tidal waters, waters that in turn are like priests for the ablution they offer the earth, earth that is in turn like a human being for needing daily to be absolved. While the sonnet thrives on the unpredictable exfoliation of its figures, the sonnet's maker wants to be steadfast. And yet, when he begins in the third quatrain to describe his unchanging state, he nonetheless deploys metaphors of temporal change: "Pillow'd upon my fair love's ripening breast."

Of course the power, the poignancy, of Keats's poem inheres in this tension. The *or* in the poem's final line offers a choice between life and death that the figure of the "ripening breast" has already blurred, and logically Keats should admit that his only choice is "to hear her tender-taken breath" *and* "swoon to death." This is the opposite of frustrating, however, for if we feel the ghostly presence of this poem's maker, who continues to speak to us even in death, it is not because we've extracted from the poem dependable conclusions. It is because, for a moment, we continue to live in the linguistic act of becoming, participating in the ongoing project of knowledge, rather than simply receiving its results.

"Pilot,—tempest, too": Crane coupled these two figures in a

Figure [59]

sonnet addressed to Shakespeare, describing his predecessor as a poet who by (as it were) steering the boat conjured the storm—as a poet whose exquisitely made poems paradoxically produced unmanageable energies. The same set of figures might be used to characterize Crane himself, but if Crane's metaphors sometimes seem more challenging even than Shakespeare's or Keats's, it is not because they are necessarily more quixotic but because the sonnets of Shakespeare and Keats distract us from the explosive energy of their figuration with their suavity of formal coherence: the poems sound whole. To understand why, we need to pay attention not only to syntax, diction, and figuration but to the way syllables may sound like one another—stresses making rhythms, phonemes making rhymes.

V

RHYTHM

The syllables of Old English poems are organized in lines, lines that have four stresses that alliterate with one another in one of several patterns.

Bitre **brēost**caere ge**bid**en **hæb**be

This line (which might be rendered as "I have abided bitter breast-cares") ends where it ends not because of how it looks but because of how it sounds; the pattern made by the alliterating stressed syllables is complete. This sonic patterning is so strong that when Old English poems were first written down, their lines did not need to be registered visually on the page: the poems were transcribed as if they were prose. Greek and Latin poems were also written down as if they were prose; nobody ever saw the shape of a Sapphic stanza until an editor arranged Sappho's lines on the page, offering obvious visual cues for the sonic patterning of her lines.

In contrast, Shakespeare's way of organizing the sound of Modern English into iambic pentameter lines (lines that contain five stressed syllables that do not necessarily alliterate but have a particular relationship to the unstressed syllables surrounding them) was always registered visually on the page.

> **Let** me **not** to the **mar**riage of **true minds**
> Admit impediments.

We nevertheless recognize the first ten syllables of this sentence as a variation of the iambic pentameter line not because of how they look; we recognize the line because of how the syllables sound in relationship to one another, just as Shakespeare made the line by listening to how they sound.

Yet our now established habit of looking at poems, fostered by the rise of print culture, has altered the way poets think about the sound of poetry. Beginning in the later seventeenth century, poets we call Augustan or neoclassical grew to prefer a smoother pentameter line, free of the adventurous rhythmic variations of Shakespeare and Donne, as if the line's neatness of finish were a reflection of its appearance on the printed page; John Crowe Ransom was harkening back to these neoclassical tastes when he called Shakespeare's sonnets ill-constructed. More recently, the habit of looking at poems has encouraged the production of a flaccid free-verse line whose length is determined merely by its visual relationship to other lines on the page. Just as it seems logical that films will change if we expect to watch them on an iPad rather than in a movie theater, poems have changed because of the changing technologies through which the English language has been experienced, print being the most obvious. What electronic media will do to poetry remains largely to be seen.

But what is more remarkable is the fact that, over hundreds of years, poetry in English has changed so little. The pentameter line, which eclipsed the alliterative four-beat line deployed by Old English poets, was developed in response to the prosody of French poems that entered the ears of Middle English writers along with the French language itself. It would be difficult to wedge Latinate words like *impediments* or *pilgrimage* into the Old English line even if those words had been available to Old English poets, and as Middle English settled into Modern English, the pentameter became essential not only to Shakespeare but to Pope, Keats, and Stevens. The line remains essential to innumerable poets writing in English today, but this continuity of formal procedure is a symptom of a deeper continuity, one that also underlies the disruptive formal procedures of innumerable poets writing today.

Consider Ezra Pound's "In a Station of the Metro," one of the foundational free-verse poems in English.

> The apparition of these faces in the crowd;
> Petals on a wet, black bough.

Each of these lines is made from a combination of Latinate and Germanic diction; the Latinate nouns tend to be multisyllabic (*apparition, petal*), while the Germanic nouns tend to be monosyllables (*crowd, bough*), as do the function words that English syntax requires (*of, these, in, on*). Syntactically, the poem consists of a sequence of prepositional phrases (*of these faces, in a crowd, on a wet*); there is no predication, no verb, but by suggesting a metaphorical equivalence, the semicolon asks to be understood as a copulative verb (*these faces are petals*) or as a copulative verb plus a preposition (*these faces are like petals*).

How do this diction and syntax generate the poem's rhythm? In the first line, the multisyllabic word *apparition* is necessarily pronounced *apparition*—two unstressed syllables followed by a stressed syllable and an unstressed syllable. The subsequent function words aren't generally stressed in English unless something directs us to do so. Tension between syntax and line may produce that direction—

> The apparition of these faces in
> The crowd

—thereby throwing emphasis on an otherwise unstressed preposition; but Pound's poem offers no such direction, leaving us to stress the more semantically charged nouns, as the function words fall away.

> The appa**ri**tion of these **fac**es in the **crowd**

Since the nine unstressed syllables in this line are broken into three groups of three, each group followed by a stressed syllable, it seems the poem may possibly be establishing a regular rhythmic pattern, one that might be repeated—*ti ti ti **tum** ti ti ti **tum** ti ti ti **tum***. We won't know if that's true, however, until we listen to the second line. Pound is famous for being one of the inventors of free verse in English, but he also wrote artfully metrical verse throughout his entire career.

In the second line, the multisyllabic word *petals* is necessarily pronounced *petals*, and, once again, the function words following this noun remain unstressed ("**Pet**als on a"). This little string of unstressed syllables throws us forward into the more semantically charged adjectives and noun concluding the line ("wet, black bough"), which turns out to sound nothing like the first line.

Petals on a **wet, black bough**

This density of stressed syllables feels emphatic in itself, and the density is reinforced by the rhyme of "wet" with the first syllable of "petals," the alliteration of "black" with "bough," and, most importantly, by the way in which the second line's irregular rhythm (***tum** ti ti ti **tum tum tum***) disrupts the regularity of the first (*ti ti ti **tum** ti ti ti **tum** ti ti ti **tum***). The whole poem delivers us into the concluding triplet of stresses.

Describing this delivery, I didn't presume Pound's poem to be metered or unmetered; I listened to the relationship of its stressed and unstressed syllables, noted patterns where patterns emerged, and concluded that the poem was more invested in disrupting rhythmic patterns than sustaining them. But when I listen to a poem Lord Byron wrote in the winter of 1817, when the extravagances of the Venetian *carnevale* had given way to the deprivations of Lent, I conclude that the relationship of stressed and unstressed syllables follows a metrical pattern sustained line by line: every line contains three beats, and most lines are iambic (*ti **tum** ti **tum** ti **tum***), though many lines begin with an extra unstressed syllable ("And the **moon** be **still** as **bright**") and some lines both begin and end with an extra unstressed syllable ("Though the **heart** be **still** as **lov**ing").

> So, we'll go no more a roving
>   So late into the night,
> Though the heart be still as loving,
>   And the moon be still as bright.

> For the sword outwears its sheath,
>   And the soul wears out the breast,
> And the heart must pause to breathe,
>   And love itself have rest.
>
> Though the night was made for loving,
>   And the day returns too soon,
> Yet we'll go no more a roving
>   By the light of the moon.

Sometimes the pattern of these three-beat lines asks us to stress syllables we might not ordinarily stress (such as the second syllable of the preposition "into" in "So **late** in**to** the **night**"); other times the pattern asks us to withhold the stress on syllables we might ordinarily emphasize (such as the verb "wears" in the line "And the **soul** wears **out** its **breast**"). In these lines, the pleasure of the repeated pattern threatens to trump the way in which we'd more naturally pronounce the phases containing these words: the poem, as Robert Frost said memorably of metered poems at large, breaks "the sounds of sense with all their irregularity of accent against the regular beat of the meter."

But if pattern sometimes threatens to subsume variation, the final line of Byron's poem is so rhythmically irregular—

By the **light** of the **moon**

—that our ears are able to hear it as a three-beat iambic line only by stressing the function word "of" and by inserting a pause [x] where an unstressed syllable should appear.

By the **light** [x] **of** the **moon**

Our ears crave this way of hearing the line, but the rhythm of the line itself (*ti ti **tum** ti ti **tum***) forces us to resist this way of hearing it—especially because Byron's syntax, working with his lineation, helps to generate the rhythm. While his more metrically regular second stanza features four independent clauses connected paratactically, each clause complete on its line (*for the sword . . . and the soul . . . and the heart . . . and love itself*), the final stanza shifts to hypotaxis: the opening subordinate clause ("Though the **night** was **made** for **lov**ing") suddenly propels us toward the stanza's concluding independent clause, which is itself energized by enjambment, throwing us into the final line's disruptive rhythm.

> Yet we'll **go** no **more** a **rov**ing
> By the **light** of the **moon**.

Experienced within the context of Byron's meticulously managed sonic decorum, this small rhythmic variation feels momentous. Just as our experience of a poem depends not simply on the presence of different kinds of syntax, diction, or figuration, so does our experience depend not simply on the presence of rhythmic variation but on the way in which we move through the poem to discover the variation. There are as many paths to discovery as there are poems.

Both Byron's and Pound's poems look the way we've come to expect poems to look on the page: line-endings provide visual cues for the sonic duration of the lines. Not only were Old English poems written down without line-endings, however; as M. B. Parkes reminds us in his history of punctuation, they were written down without punctuation, and punctuation remained wildly erratic for centuries to come. Today, we're used to reading the sixteenth-century poet Sir Thomas Wyatt in editions in which punctuation offers visual cues for the syntactical relationship of clauses and phrases, just as it does in Byron or Pound, but Wyatt's original texts often contain no punctuation at all.

> It may be good like it who list
> but I do dowbt who can me blame
> for oft assured yet have I myst
> and now again I fere the same

Despite the lack of punctuation, it's easy to hear that this quatrain is written in four-beat, mostly iambic lines ("But **I** do **dowbt** who **can** me **blame**"), lines that sometimes contain the same kind of run-on syntax we found in Ellen Bryant Voigt's unpunctuated "Sleep": "I am exhausted a coma looks good to me." But that rhythmic momentum is due to the line, working against the syntax, not to the lack of punctuation as such. Were the syntax lineated this way, with or without punctuation—

> It may be good
> like it who list
> but I do dowbt
> who can me blame

—the poem's animating rhythmic life would disappear: the duration of the lines and the duration of the clauses and phrases are in every case identical.

Wyatt was following the conventions of his time, not flouting them, in his eschewal of punctuation. Notoriously, Emily Dickinson ignored the conventions of her time, avoiding print publication and setting down her poems by hand in unconventional ways. This is how one of her poems first appeared on the page after her death: spelling, punctuation, and lineation have been regularized, the first line altered, and the final two lines of the poem deleted.

> He fumbles at your spirit
>> As players at the keys
> Before they drop full music on;
>> He stuns you by degrees,
>
> Prepares your brittle substance
>> For the ethereal blow,
> By fainter hammers, further heard,
>> Then nearer, then so slow
>
> Your breath has time to straighten,
>> Your brain to bubble cool,—
> Deals one imperial thunderbolt
>> That scalps your naked soul.

This editorially imposed punctuation and lineation attempt to provide visual cues for the poem's rhythmic life. While some lines are inevitably more regular than others, the metrical pattern asks us to hear four beats in the third line of each stanza ("By **faint**er **ham**mers, **fur**ther **heard**"), while the first, second, and fourth lines contain three ("Then **near**er, **then** so **slow**"). The generally iambic meter inevitably fights the natural rhythms of the syntax in some lines ("As **play**ers **at** the **key**"), and in the penultimate line this tension rises to its greatest intensity: that is, our ears want to hear the line not as "Deals **one** im**per**ial **thun**der**bolt**" but as "**Deals one** im**per**ial **thun-**

derbolt," the opening monosyllabic verb begging to be stressed and the proliferation of unstressed syllables in the concluding noun begging to fall away. Because the two lines preceding this dramatically disruptive line begin with the same unstressed function word ("Your **breath**"—"Your **brain**"), our urge to stress the semantically charged verb *deals* becomes all the more prominent: "**Deals one.**"

In what ways do Dickinson's idiosyncratic punctuation and lineation change the way we hear the poem's language? This is how a recent edition of her poems attempts to replicate Dickinson's lines as she wrote them: the metrical pattern and rhyme scheme is unemphasized by stanza breaks, and the punctuation is not generally grammatical (organizing the sense) but rhetorical (marking the rhythms of the syntax as it is organized in lines).

> He fumbles at your Soul
> As Players at the Keys
> Before they drop full Music on—
> He stuns you by degrees—
> Prepares your brittle nature
> For the Etherial Blow
> By fainter Hammers—further heard—
> Then nearer—Then so slow
> Your Breath has time to straighten—
> Your brain—to bubble Cool—
> Deals—One—imperial—Thunderbolt—
> That scalps your naked Soul—

Reading this more accurate transcription of the poem, our ears still want to hear the penultimate line's rhythm as a dramatic disruption of an established pattern ("**Deals one** im**per**ial **thun**-derbolt"), and Dickinson's punctuation makes the disruptive rhythm of the line more emphatically clear: the grammatically unnecessary dashes separating the first three syllables ("**Deals—One**—im**per**ial—**Thun**derbolt") alert us to this line's bold turn from the previous lines' more regular iambs ("Your **brain**—to **bub**ble **Cool**"). But however powerful Dickinson's punctuation, what we are hearing is the rhythm of English diction and syntax organized in lines, just as we hear it in the line "**Pet**als on a **wet**, **black**, **bough**" or in the line "By the **light** of the **moon**."

As a medium for poetry, the English language is distinguished by the contrast of words with etymologically distant roots, by a syntax requiring lots of unstressed function words, our nouns and verbs having long ago lost most of their inflections, and by the fact that the meaning of our nouns and verbs depends on syllable stress. Because of the nature of the medium, lines in our poems came to be organized by the relationship of stressed to unstressed syllables, and, over time, our ways of noting that organization visually have become part of the poetic medium as well. But while it's possible to write a poem without line-endings or punctuation, it's impossible to write a poem without deploying diction and syntax. The rhythmic power of any particular line depends on how we're asked to hear its diction and syntax in the dynamic context of a particular poem, no matter if it looks like prose on the page, no matter if we call it formal or free. The medium is more powerful than the maker, as every maker knows.

VI

ECHO

Listen again to the second quatrain of Shakespeare's twelfth sonnet.

> When lofty trees I see barren of leaves,
> Which erst from heat did canopy the herd,
> And summer's green all girded up in sheaves
> Borne on the bier with white and bristly beard . . .

The syllables at the ends of these metrical lines sound like one another, though *leaves* sounds closer to *sheaves* than *herd* does to *beard*, at least to twenty-first-century ears. At the same time, syllables echo one another within the lines. In the line "Borne on the bier with white and bristly beard," the syllable *beard* shares an initial consonant with *borne* and *bristly* and, more forcefully, *beard* shares an initial consonant and vowel sound with *bier*; the syllable *white* stands alone. Why does Shakespeare hold back from extending the pattern of repeated sounds? Why not *borne on the bier with bright and bristly bier*?

Poets revel in the interplay of similar and dissimilar sounds in part because the effectiveness of any language as a method for communication depends on such interplay. We recognize the meaning of the word *bed* because we're able to differentiate its sound from the sounds of the words *beard* and *dead* and *board* and *red*, and sometimes words may sound so similar that their meaning is obscured. A slip of the tongue or a distracted ear might encourage us to mistake *bed* for *board* or *beard* for *bier*; only the context of a particular utterance will tell us whether we're hearing the word *board* or the word *bored*. Infamously, the line "oh no, me gotta go" in the '60s pop song "Louie Louie" was heard as "grab her way down low," prompting a lengthy FBI investigation into the song's possible obscenity.

In daily conversation we might find such slippage merely confusing, but when we hear similar-sounding words echoing one another in poems, often (but not always) we call it rhyme. We don't generally refer to *bier* and *beard* as rhymes because, by long consensus, a rhyme involves the repetition of a vowel sound and a concluding consonant. By similarly long consensus, we've come to expect that kind of echo at the ends of a poem's lines.

But not by very long consensus. Though the lines of Old English poems were organized by the kind of echo we call alliteration, they were not rhymed. Neither were Greek and Latin poems rhymed. Beginning in the eleventh century, however, as the new French fashion for rhyming poems began to enter English, the challenge of rhyme came increasingly to distinguish English-language poems as poems. By the time Milton wrote *Paradise Lost* without rhyme in the seventeenth century, some intelligent readers didn't know what to make of it.

Today, unrhymed and unmetered poems have been acceptable in English for more than a century, but a certain proportion of our words of course continue to echo one another; the word *bed* still sounds like the words *beard* and *dead*, and the vitality of our poems still depends on such echoes, whether they're rhymed or not, just as the vitality of our poems still depends on the relationship of stressed and unstressed syllables, whether they're metered or not. To say that this quatrain rhymes—

> He fumbles at your Soul
> As Players at the Keys
> Before they drop full Music on—
> He stuns you by degrees—

—and that this quatrain also rhymes—

> So, we'll go no more a roving
> So late into the night,
> Though the heart be still as loving,
> And the moon be still as bright

—is not to have said very much about the sonic life of these poems. But to notice that four of the seven words in the first line of Byron's quatrain play on the same vowel sound (*so, go, no, roving*) is to recognize that, even if Byron's quatrain were not rhymed at all, its syllables would echo one another more densely than Dickinson's. While every poem is made from syllables that sound like one another and syllables that sound different, Dickinson's leans slightly more toward difference. Byron's leans toward similarity, which is why one might say that his quatrain sounds a bit more like song and a bit less like prose.

Strictly speaking, I'm using the word *echo* metaphorically, since the word refers to the reflection of sound waves off solid surfaces; certainly I'm using the words *song* and *prose* metaphorically, since a prose sentence may be packed with syllables that echo one another, making it seem songlike—as this passage from a sermon by John Donne reveals. Donne is making here a comparison between Greek and Christian attitudes toward the afterlife.

> The Gentils, and their Poets, describe the sad state of Death so, *Nox una obeunda*, That it is one of everlasting Night; To them, a Night; But to a Christian, it is *Dies Mortis,* and *Dies Resurrectionis*, The day of Death, and The day of Resurrection; We die in the light, in the sight of Gods presence, and we rise in the light, in the sight of his very Essence.

The final twenty-five syllables of this sentence are made from twenty-three words; only two words, "presence" and "absence," have more than one syllable. If you lineate these twenty-five syllables by paying attention to the natural rhythm of the syntax (which features a sequence of prepositional phrases) and by paying attention also to the way in which the more highly stressed nouns and verbs echo one another (*die, light, sight, rise*), you get an eight-line poem rhymed *abbc abbc*, a poem mostly in anapestic monometer (ti ti **tum** / ti ti **tum**).

> We die
> in the light,
> in the sight
> of Gods presence,

> and we rise
> in the light,
> in the sight
> of his very Essence.

These syllables are as rife with echo as comparable passages from many poems, rhymed or unrhymed.

In fact, they are so rife with echo that the effect, when emphasized by lineation, may feel a little overdone: once our ears register the metrical regularity of Donne's sentence, the fact that every prominently stressed syllable rhymes with other stressed syllables feels overly predictable. Similarly, if all five stressed syllables alliterated with one another in Shakespeare's line "Borne on the bier with white and bristly beard," the line would lose its vitality: "Borne on the bier with bright and bristly beard." If the density of sonic echo in Byron's first line ("So, we'll go no more a roving") continued in the second line ("In the morning all aglow"), the poem would sound sentimental rather than poignantly sincere.

Sometimes a poet may covet such effects, as in these self-consciously excessive lines from Algernon Charles Swinburne's "Nephelidia"—

From the depth of the dreamy decline of the dawn through a
    notable nimbus of nebulous noonshine

—or from Wallace Stevens's "Bantams in Pine-Woods."

> Chieftain Iffucan of Azcan in caftan
> Of tan with henna hackles, halt!

An abundance of echo tends to reduce discourse to incanta-
tion, song to jingle, sense to nonsense, and sometimes a poet
may covet this effect as well.

> Mallah walla tella bella. Trah mah trah-la, la-la-la,
> Mah la belle. Ippa Fano wanna bella, wella-wah.

These are the first two lines of Robert Pinsky's "Gulf Music,"
a poem occasioned by the devastation of the city of New Orleans by Hurricane Katrina in the fall of 2005. These are the
second two lines.

> The hurricane of September 8, 1900 devastated
> Galveston, Texas. Some 8,000 people died.

The extremes are energetic here, as if the subtle interplay of similar and dissimilar sounds in a line like "Borne on the bier with
white and bristly beard" were turned into a contest between
song and *prose*. Not many poems sound as flatly informative
as "8,000 people died," the lines avoiding as much echo as the
medium allows, and not many poems sound as fecklessly nonsensical as "Trah mah trah-la, la-la-la," the lines embracing a sur-
feit of echo with even more appetite than Stevens.

Yet the extremes are deceptive, for as these syllables are
repeated throughout the poem, what sounds like nonsense
begins increasingly to make sense, *trah mah* congealing as *try
my*: *try my tra, la, la*—which is what the New Orleans piano-
player Professor Longhair seems to be saying in "Tipitina," a
song that plays apparently nonsensical lyrics against the familiar chord progression of an eight-bar blues. Between refrain-like
repetitions of Professor Longhair's almost indecipherable syl-

lables, the informational lines of "Gulf Music" veer from the obliteration of Galveston to Pinsky's great-grandfather Morris Eisenberg (who in 1908 was given his first name by an immigration officer in Galveston and who later took his surname from a rich man in Arkansas) to Professor Longhair himself (whose given name was Henry Roeland Byrd) to Pinsky's great-grandmother Becky, who abandoned her daughter Pearl (named for the Pearl City of Galveston) to run off with Morris Eisenberg (who had the same surname as Pearl's father). The poem's information is revealed increasingly to have been determined by a coincidence of sounds.

This revelation does not challenge the stable ground on which information stands, however, but reminds us that the ground was only ever more or less stable. For while we ought to remember that a devastating hurricane killed 8,000 citizens of Galveston on September 8, 1900, we won't generally reread "Gulf Music" in order to acquire this kind of knowledge, and, in any case, other sources say that as many as 12,000 people died. As "Gulf Music" also says, "the past is not decent or orderly, it is made-up and devious," a proposition that the poem's concluding lines demonstrate.

> Henry formed a group named Professor Longhair and his
> Shuffling Hungarians. After so much renunciation
>
> And invention, is this the image of the promised end?
> All music haunted by all the music of the dead forever.
>
> Becky haunted forever by Pearl the daughter she abandoned
> For love, O try my tra-la-la, ma la belle, mah walla-woe.

These lines veer from Shakespeare's vision of King Lear carrying the dead body of his daughter Cordelia ("Is this the promised end? / Or image of that horror?"), to the apparent nonsense which the poem has repeated multiple times—except that the nonsense now seems more meaningful than ever, just as the information has come to seem driven by sound. "O try my tra-la-la" may be the song of the lover, the panderer, or the dealer, but whatever it is, it is also the song of Orpheus, desperate to raise the dead.

Describing syntax, diction, figuration, and rhythm, I've argued that what matters is not simply the presence of Germanic and Latinate diction, paratactic and hypotactic syntax, figurative and literal language, or rhythmically regular and irregular lines. What matters is that the final sentence of Moore's "My Apish Cousins" moves from Latinate to Germanic diction, that the first stanza of Donne's "The Canonization" moves from parataxis to hypotaxis, that Shakespeare's twelfth sonnet moves from conventional to extravagant metaphors, that Pound's "In a Station of the Metro" moves from a rhythmically regular line to an irregular line.

As the juxtapositions of "Gulf Music" make emphatically clear, echo plays out in the same way: our experience of a poem is determined by the way we're made to move between different degrees of echo as the poem's language unfolds. The final line of Stevens's late poem "Of Mere Being" ("The bird's fire-fangled feathers dangle down") feels revelatory because it leaps to a density of echo to which the preceding lines do not contribute.

> The palm stands on the edge of space.
> The wind moves slowly in the branches.
> The bird's fire-fangled feathers dangle down.

And the final line of Stevens's late poem "Not Ideas about the Thing but the Thing Itself" ("A new knowledge of reality") feels revelatory because it suddenly refuses to participate in the swirling web of similar sounds (*precede, sun, surround, still—cry, chorister, choir, colossal*) from which it is extruded.

> That scrawny cry—it was
> A chorister whose c preceded the choir.
> It was part of the colossal sun,
>
> Surrounded by its choral rings,
> Still far away. It was like
> A new knowledge of reality.

Reading lines like "A chorister whose c preceded the choir" or "The bird's fire-fangled feathers dangle down," we feel a density of similar sounds, but, more importantly, we feel the poems moving toward or away from that density, just as we may also feel a poem's rhythm moving toward or away from regularity or a poem's syntax moving toward or away from the drama of subordination.

This sonic drama may transpire on a small scale (a single line from Shakespeare's twelfth sonnet) or on a large scale (the juxtaposed couplets of "Gulf Music"), but every poem feels unique because the language of every poem is performing multiple actions at once, creating a repeatable path of discovery—a new knowledge of reality—through the simultaneous ordering of different degrees of echo, different kinds of syntax, different kinds of diction, different levels of figuration, and different degrees of rhythmic regularity.

VII

IMAGE

"The three fundamental colors are red, yellow, blue," wrote Vincent van Gogh to his brother Theo.

> The whole chemistry of colors is no more complicated than those simple few fundamentals. And a good understanding of them is worth more than 70 different shades of paint—given that more than 70 tones and strengths can be made with the 3 primary colors and white and black. The colorist is he who on seeing a color in nature is able to analyze it coolly and say, for example, that green-grey is yellow with black and almost no blue, &c.

This is an artist describing his intimacy with his medium. The painter who would replicate the colors in nature must analyze them coolly, and the painting itself is produced through his understanding of how the fundamental elements of the medium may be manipulated.

"Go in fear of abstractions," said Pound in one of the manifestos associated with the Imagist movement in poetry, which flourished in the second decade of the twentieth century. Pound wanted to encourage poets to emphasize the concrete, generally Germanic diction of the English language, though he himself was not shy about deploying abstractions. "Do not be descriptive," Pound added: "remember that the painter can describe a landscape much better than you can." This remark is also borne of an artist's intimacy with his medium; paintings have colors, poems have words for colors. How then could a poem be described as being made of *images*? And how could a painting be said to *describe* a landscape? Pound's verb suggests that a desire for the scribal, the written, may sneak into our sense of the visual, just as a desire for the visual may infect our sense of the written.

More than once Pound told the story of how he came to write "In a Station of the Metro," which is a story about translating a visual experience into a verbal experience: exiting from the Concorde station in Paris one day in 1911, he saw a beautiful face, then another and another, then a child's face, then the face of a beautiful woman.

> I tried all that day to find words for what this had meant to me, and I could not find any words that seemed to me worthy, or as lovely as that sudden emotion. And that evening, as I went home along the Rue Raynouard, I was still trying, and I found, suddenly, the expression . . . not in speech, but in little splotches of colour. . . . I wrote a thirty-line poem, and destroyed it because it was what we call

work "of second intensity." Six months later I made
a poem half that length.

Thirty lines, fifteen lines: Pound finally produced the two lines
of "In a Station of the Metro" after another year of toil. While
the visual experience transpired in seconds, the process of finding the right words took eighteen months: "Petals on a wet,
black bough."

A poet might observe in the world a beautiful image, just as
a poet might learn an arresting fact or think of a challenging
idea. But as Pound's story suggests, a poem we call imagistic is
made of words bound together by a web of sonic patterns. Those
words may in turn provoke a mental image, but while brain and
cognitive scientists debate the nature of such images, the "pic-
torialists" arguing that they're more like pictures, the "descrip-
tionists" maintaining that they're more like language, both
camps agree that their own language is metaphorical: "Brain
scientists have found no pictures in the brain," emphasizes the
philosopher Ned Block.

Neither has anyone ever found a picture in a poem, just as
no one has ever actually heard a voice; when applied to poetry,
the word *image* is also metaphorical, part of a web of metaphors
we use regularly to describe the elusive process of thinking as
an instantly apprehensible visual process—we *reflect* or *speculate*
on things that have *brilliance* or *clarity*; we say *I see* when we
understand. It's understandably seductive to think of poems as
being made of images, just as it's seductive to think of a poem as
having a voice; but like what we call the poetic voice, the poetic
image is constructed from the more fundamental aspects of the
medium—diction, syntax, figure, rhythm, echo.

These free-verse lines by William Carlos Williams—

> Her body is not so white as
> anemone petals nor so smooth—nor
> so remote a thing. It is a field
> of the wild carrot taking
> the field by force

—and these metered and rhymed lines by W. H. Auden—

> As I walked out one evening,
>   Walking down Bristol Street,
> The crowds upon the pavement
>   Were fields of harvest wheat.

—foreground their occasion as an observable event, making us feel intimate with the poet's act of evoking the visual world in concrete diction: *a field of harvest wheat, a field of wild carrot.* But both poems deploy this diction as part of a metaphor— *the crowds were fields of harvest wheat, her body is a field of wild carrot.* How do you picture a body simultaneously as a field? An act of thinking, not an act of description, is required to sustain that simultaneity.

Often the power of poems we tend to call imagistic (whether they're written before or after Pound) depends on the strategic suppression of such thinking—on the suppression, that is, of figurative language and hypotactic syntax. Ben Jonson, writing in the early seventeenth century.

> Ha' you felt the wool o' the beaver?
>   Or swansdown ever?

> Or have smelt o' the bud o' the briar?
>   Or the nard in the fire?
> Or have tasted the bag of the bee?

C. D. Wright, writing in the late twentieth century.

the breath	the trees	the bridge
the road	the rain	the sheen
the breath	the line	the skin
the vineyard	the fences	the leg
the water	the breath	the shift

Both these poems attempt to foreground sensuous experience at the expense of syntactical activity. Verbs in Jonson's poem serve merely to present a paratactic list of sensuous delights, and in Wright's poem verbs have fallen away, leaving an even more unmediated juxtaposition of nouns—a poetic structure that, in the wake of the Imagist movement, twentieth-century readers often likened to the visual experience of collage. Since both Wright's and Jonson's poems are about erotic delight, the strategy feels cumulatively powerful: we don't need much *why* when the tumbling forward of the *what* is so satisfying.

But the poems can sustain this blissed-out thoughtlessness only for so long. Jonson's final line makes it clear that he has not simply been cataloguing the delight of swan's down and honey but making an argument about the beauty of a particular woman: the down and honey are not images but metaphors—

"O so sweet is she!" Wright's final line also leaps to figuration, reinforcing the leap with an unprecedented excess of similar sounds, and making it clear that her poem has all along been building a narrative of dangerously irresistible sexual attraction.

the mouth	the tongue	the eyes
the burn	the burned	the burning

Wright's poem may seem idiosyncratic, but it's difficult to find a poet from the last hundred years who remained untouched by the Imagist Pound's preference for concrete diction and juxtapositional logic. Reinforcing the pronouncements of the Imagist manifestos, the young T. S. Eliot argued even more influentially that poems should be made of what he called "objective correlatives"—which was another way of saying *go in fear of abstractions*: rather than proclaiming that *your body is not only beautiful but seductively assertive in its beauty*, a poet might say *you are a field of wild carrot taking the field by force*, offering the concrete product of a process of thought. Eliot often cited a favorite line by John Donne as an example of such powerfully concrete language—

A bracelet of bright hair about the bone

—and one can sense right away that the vocabulary of "image" and "objective correlative" would allow us to admire poets as different from each other as Shakespeare—

Borne on the bier with white and bristly beard

—and Wright.

the burn   the burned   the burning

Yet it's crucial to notice, as Eliot would not have denied, that each of these is a successful *line* of poetry because of how it sounds. Each line is rhythmically distinctive, and each line is bound tightly to itself by a web of similar sounds. Crucially, what might be in danger of sounding like an excess of alliteration in each line (*bracelet, bright, bone—borne, bier, bristly, beard—burn, burned, burning*) is tempered by the way in which each poem delivers us to that excess.

> And he that digs it spies
> A bracelet of bright hair about the bone
> *
> And summer's green all girded up in sheaves
> Borne on the bier with white and bristly beard
> *
> the mouth   the tongue   the eyes
> the burn   the burned   the burning

In each poem, the poet brings us to a line rich in echo with lines that share none of that richness. As I've emphasized, our experience of these poems is shaped not simply by the presence of particular elements of the medium but the order in which those elements appear. And what we call a line made of images would not be successful if the line did not simultaneously, in relationship to other lines, construct and disrupt a dynamically unfolding pattern of sounds.

The same is true of a line made exclusively of abstract language. Even if we recognize that our vocabulary of the poetic image is metaphorical, a way of speaking about linguistic processes as visual processes, the potential danger of the vocabulary is that it might encourage us to assume that poems harnessing abstract diction are automatically less successful than poems made of concrete diction. How do we describe the power of poems by William Blake—

> Pity would be no more,
> If we did not make somebody Poor

—or Susan Howe—

> Great emptiness as
> simple as that went
> So straight before

—or the later Eliot—

> Time present and time past
> Are both perhaps present in time future

—poems that, different as they are from each other, would never be described as made of images? While the younger Eliot of "Prufrock" and the "objective correlative" championed a poetry of concrete images, the later Eliot did not go in fear of abstractions; his best friends were abstractions.

Just as what we call an imagistic poem must pay scrupulous attention to the sonic drama of its syllables unfolding in time,

so must the poem of abstract thinking run on the rails of its
diction, syntax, rhythm, and echo.

Pity would be no more
If we did not make somebody Poor:
And Mercy no more could be,
If all were as happy as we;

And mutual fear brings peace;
Till the selfish loves increase.
Then Cruelty knits a snare,
And spreads his baits with care.

He sits down with holy fears,
And waters the ground with tears:
Then Humility takes its root
Underneath his foot.

Soon spreads the dismal shade
Of Mystery over his head;
And the Catterpiller and Fly
Feed on the Mystery.

And it bears the fruit of Deceit,
Ruddy and sweet to eat;
And the Raven his nest has made
In its thickest shade.

The Gods of the earth and sea,
Sought thro' Nature to find this Tree

But their search was all in vain:
There grows one in the Human Brain.

While only two lines of Blake's "The Human Abstract" scan effortlessly as iambic trimeters ("And **spreads** his **baits** with **care**"—"Soon **spreads** the **dis**mal **shade**"), the remaining twenty-two lines play with this three-beat pattern, offering a tireless variety of variations but never obliterating the metrical pattern's force: sometimes we're asked to stress syllables we'd ordinarily demote ("**In** its **thick**est **shade**"), and sometimes we're asked to suppress syllables we'd ordinarily emphasize ("Sought thro' **Na**ture to **find** this **Tree**"). While the poem's lines are almost exclusively end-stopped, and while these syntactically complete lines veer aggressively toward the epigrammatic, no two consecutive lines are rhythmically identical.

Figuration enters the poem in the second stanza, personifying the abstract entities (pity, mercy, fear, love, cruelty) that have so far dominated every clause: cruelty *knits a snare, spreads his baits, waters the grounds*; humility *takes its root, spreads dismal shade*. Blake strings his figures together with parallel syntax, as he often does, and in "The Human Abstract" this continuity of syntactical procedures encourages us not to notice how the vehicles of the metaphors increasingly take charge of the poem: rather than thinking about the sinister self-congratulation built into acts of pity and mercy, we're imagining the dense shade of a tree, in which a raven has made his nest.

But if we're tempted to think of this tree as an image, rather than a metaphor, Blake's final stanza stops us short: having searched nature for this tree, with its raven, caterpillar, and fly, even the gods must admit that it is a mental construction; unlike the growth of trees, human suffering is not natural or inevitable. The poem's final line delivers this wisdom almost like a punch line ("There grows one in the Human Brain"), and the punch is rhythmic: like the final line of Byron's "So, we'll go no more a roving," this line deviates so far from the poem's metrical pattern that we cannot hear it as "There grows **one** in the **hum**an **brain**." We need to punch out those monosyllables, which refuse to lie quietly: "There **grows one** in the **hum**an **brain**."

What is the wish for poems to be made of images a wish for? At best, like the wish for a poem to have a voice, it is a wish for immediacy, a wish that poems by Jonson, Williams, and Wright repay handsomely. But at worst, it is a wish for the reassuring ground of empirical knowledge rather than the dynamic process of lyric knowledge—a wish that, if it were fulfilled, would make the poem's language feel disposable rather than inexhaustible. The Imagist Pound suggested that landscape should be left to painters, because of the nature of their medium. But even a Van Gogh painting is not made of images; it is made of minerals ground and mixed with linseed oil, then smeared on canvas and allowed to cure.

VIII

REPETITION

This is the first section of Mark Strand's "Elevator," a poem divided into two numbered parts, each part consisting of three end-stopped lines.

> The elevator went to the basement. The doors opened.
> A man stepped in and asked if I was going up.
> "I'm going down," I said. "I won't be going up."

This is the second section.

> The elevator went to the basement. The doors opened.
> A man stepped in and asked if I was going up.
> "I'm going down," I said. "I won't be going up."

If the order in which a poem's fundamental elements appear is crucial—diction, syntax, figuration, echo—what happens when the poem's elements are identical?

Any aspect of the medium might be repeated in a poem.

Phonemes may be repeated, words may be repeated, entire lines, phrases, or clauses may be repeated. But more crucially, the power of any particular instance of repetition (or any particular instance of variation) may be doubled when it coincides with another instance. We've seen that Shakespeare's twelfth sonnet generates great structural power by reinforcing a pattern of syntactical repetition with a pattern of lineation: the repetitions are synchronized.

> When I do count the clock . . .
> When I behold the violet . . .
> When lofty trees I see . . .

And similarly we've seen that the repeated phonemes larding John Donne's prose sentence (*die, light, sight, rise*) become much more prominent when those repetitions are synchronized with a pattern of lineation that foregrounds a repeated pattern of syntax.

> We die
> in the light,
> in the sight . . .
> and we rise
> in the light,
> in the sight

Strand's "Elevator" may seem like a special case, a poem that's all refrain, no intervening verses, but given that all poems repeat themselves, what's at issue is the degree to which a poem's various patterns of repetition are synchronized: in a refrain, every aspect of the medium that might be repeated is repeated at once.

"Is it possible," begins the first stanza of an exquisite lyric by Sir Thomas Wyatt, one of our masters of refrain. The question also ends the five-line stanza, framing three lines rhymed *aaa* (a dimeter, then a tetrameter, then a pentameter). Subsequent stanzas follow suit.

> Is it possible
> That so high debate,
> So sharp, so sore, and of such rate,
> Should end so soon and was begun so late?
> Is it possible?
>
> Is it possible
> So cruel intent,
> So hasty heat and so soon spent,
> From love to hate and thence for to relent?
> Is it possible?
>
> Is it possible
> That one may find
> Within one heart so diverse mind
> To change or turn as weather and wind?
> Is it possible?

Formally, this poem asserts that nothing changes. Each stanza consists of two questions, the first beginning with the refrain and the second consisting exclusively of the refrain; the adamancy of the first question is reinforced by three lines of steadily increasing length, each concluding rhyme (*debate, rate, late*) sounding more insistent than the last. But the accumulating effect of the poem is to make us feel that anything might change—that love may all too easily turn to hate. So when the refrain changes in the penultimate stanza to "It is possible" and in the final stanza to "All is possible," we feel not that the poem is suddenly shifting course but that the shift is confirming the poem's repeated wish for constancy. By attempting so stalwartly to stand still, the poem moves inexorably forward.

Wyatt's repetitions of rhyme, line, and syntax are synchronized: what happens when a poem refuses to align its repetitions? Having considered the unfolding drama of Marianne Moore's diction in "My Apish Cousins," let's now examine the repetitions of the poem's stanza form, which operate independently from the repetitions of its syntax. The six lines of this syllabic stanza contain 15, 16, 10, 10, 15, and 11 syllables respectively, the first line rhyming with the second and the fourth line rhyming with the sixth.

> I shall never forget—that Gilgamesh among
> the hairy carnivora—that cat with the
>
> wedge-shaped, slate-gray marks on its forelegs and the
>   resolute tail,
> astringently remarking: "They have imposed on us with
>   their pale,
>   half fledged protestations, trembling about
>   in inarticulate frenzy, saying
>   it is not for all of us to understand art, finding it
>   all so difficult, examining the thing
>
> as if it were something inconceivably arcanic, as
> symmetrically frigid as something carved out of chrysopras
>   or marble—strict with tension, malignant

in its power over us and deeper
    than the sea when it proffers flattery in exchange
        for hemp,
rye, flax, horses, platinum, timber and fur."

Hanging from the initial independent clause ("They have imposed on us") are four parallel phrases modifying the act of imposition (*trembling about, saying it is not, finding it all, examining the thing*) followed by an explosion of clauses and phrases describing how the imposed-upon *thing* is consequently made to appear (*inconceivably arcanic, symmetrically frigid, strict with tension, malignant in its power, deeper than the sea*). But in contrast to Wyatt's poem, in which the parallel clauses begin each stanza, Moore's lineation does not reinforce her syntactical repetition. At the same time, because lines of the same length do not rhyme with each other, and because the lines cut against the syntax at grammatically weak junctures, the poem's rhymes are nearly inaudible; the echo linking the line "as if it were something inconceivably arcanic, as" with the line "symmetrically frigid as something carved out of chrysopras" is as weak as possible. "My Apish Cousins" is a highly repetitive poem, but one scheme of repetition diffuses another: the pattern of lines is at odds with the pattern of the syntax, and the pattern of the rhymes is synchronized with neither the pattern of the syntax nor the pattern of the lines.

Does Moore's stanza seem contrived? Does Wyatt's? Having written syllabic poems like "My Apish Cousins" during the second decade of the twentieth century, Moore began around 1920 to write poems in free verse—poems that, in some ways, seem desperate never to repeat themselves, just as Wyatt's poem seems desperate only to repeat itself. But in other ways, these poems are also highly repetitive. "New York," an unpredictably wayward catalogue of the city's diverse qualities, consists of a list of clauses dominated by the verb *to be*; sometimes the verb is elided, as in the movement from the poem's title to its first line—

> *New York*
>
> the savage's romance,
> accreted where we need the space for commerce—
> the center of the wholesale fur trade,
> starred with tepees of ermine and peopled with foxes

—and sometimes the verb is emphasized, especially in order to be negated, as in these concluding lines of the poem.

> It is not the dime-novel exterior,
> Niagara Falls, the calico horses and the war canoe;
> it is not that "if the fur is not finer than such as one sees
>   others wear,
> one would rather be without it—"
> that estimated in raw meat and berries, we could feed the
>   universe;
> it is not the atmosphere of ingenuity,
> the otter, the beaver, the puma skins
> without shooting-irons or dogs;
> it is not the plunder,
> it is the "accessibility to experience."

"New York" does not capitalize on the repetition of line-lengths, rhymes, or stanzas, but it does foreground the repetition of a syntactical pattern (the reiteration of *it is not* shifting

powerfully back to *it is* in the poem's final line). More importantly, it synchronizes this syntactical pattern with the lineation (each new iteration of the repeated clause beginning a new
line), as the more obviously repetitive "My Apish Cousins" does
not. These repetitions allow us to feel, long before we've deduced
the poem's semantic logic, that its catalogue of disparate mate-
rials is purposeful, not merely quixotic. And when the poem
concludes, the Latinate diction of the phrase "accessibility to
experience" (quoted from Henry James) rises from the predominately Germanic diction immediately preceding it (*otter, beaver,
iron, dog, plunder*) as satisfyingly as the words *hemp, rye*, and
flax rise from the predominately Latinate diction of "My Apish
Cousins."

Moore didn't want the rigor of her free-verse poems to seem
any more or less contrived than the rigor of her syllabic poems.
Organizing her 1924 book *Observations*, she began with syllabic
poems like "My Apish Cousins," moved on to list-like free-verse
poems such as "New York," and crowned the book with an over-
500-line index that feels like the long poem in which *Observations* logically culminates—a catalogue of catalogues.

> antlet
> Antarctica
> ape, curling with an
> *Apish Cousins, My*
> Apollo
> art, arcanic
> artichoke
> artist and money
> artists, fools

What could be more predictable than the repetition of the alphabet, more confirming of our expectations? What could be more unpredictable, more inviting of our curiosity, than the alphabet? It's enticing to imagine what an antlet might have to do with Antarctica, merely because of abecedarian contiguity. But it's also enticing, when reading Wyatt, to imagine what the word *debate* has to do with the words *rate* and *late* simply because the words happen to echo one another in a stanza rhymed *aaa*. It's enticing to imagine what the question *is it possible* has to do with the question *is it possible* when it's repeated in a new stanza. It's enticing to imagine what the line *A man stepped in and asked if I was going up* has to do with the line *A man stepped in and asked if I was going up*.

"If everything in the world were completely identical," says Søren Kierkegaard in *Repetition*, "in reality there would be no repetition, because reality is only in the moment." But nothing in the world is completely identical: because the repetition of an event happens over time, not in a single moment, the repeated event is altered. This is why the infamously repetitive Gertrude Stein could insist that "there can be no repetition." This is why the narrator of Jorge Luis Borges's "Pierre Menard, Author of the Quixote," can argue with deadpan plausibility that Menard's word-for-word replication of *Don Quixote* is "almost infinitely richer" than the original.

Strand's "Elevator," a Borgesian extravagance in miniature, seems to be completely static; unavailable to it is the kind of animating shift in diction that distinguishes the conclusions of both "My Apish Cousins" and "New York." But when the poem is experienced over time, it enacts a progression as much as Wyatt's poem does. For if "Elevator" consisted merely of one iteration of its three-line stanza, the scene recounted there would seem merely grim; the man riding the elevator is mortal, going down for the last time.

> The elevator went to the basement. The doors opened.
> A man stepped in and asked if I was going up.
> "I'm going down," I said. "I won't be going up."

But once the three-line stanza is repeated, the drama becomes more clearly a reflection of the sensibility of a man who expects every trip to be his last, and, as a result, the second part of the poem becomes comically poignant—an account of how we go on living, not of how we die. The man riding the elevator is mortal, like all of us, but he's not going down quite as efficiently as he pretends; he reaches the basement, and then he reaches it again. His life consists exclusively of lyric knowledge—of the eager reanimation of what he already knows.

"Elevator" does blatantly what all lyric poems do: it repeats itself so that it might also change, making us feel that our experience of the language of the poem is an event in itself—not merely the recounting of an event that happened in the past but an event we want to experience again in the present. Depending on the degree to which multiple schemes of repetition are synchronized, working either with or against one another, some poems lean more toward the pole of difference ("New York") while others lean toward the pole of sameness ("Elevator"), but every lyric poem repeats itself; every lyric poem discovers that it is different from itself. As Freud reminds us, there's something primal about the desire to repeat—as if we couldn't believe ourselves fully to be existing in the present if we weren't able to reenact the past, altering ourselves in the process. Memory is not enough.

Strand's "Elevator" gratifies this desire hyperbolically; but lest such gratification seem more droll than primal, consider two stanzas from the anonymous eighteenth-century ballad known as "The Gypsy Laddie" or "Black Jack Davey."

> Pull off, pull off them high-heeled shoes
> All made of Spanish leather.
> Get behind me on my horse,
> And we'll ride off together.
> We'll both ride off together.

> Well, she pulled off them high-heeled shoes
> All made of Spanish leather,
> Got behind him on his horse,
> And they rode off together.
> They both rode off together.

"Black Jack Davey" has been recorded several dozen times, beginning in the 1930s; I'm quoting the version recorded more recently by Pete Seeger and Bob Dylan. Ballads are distinguished generally by the alternation of tetrameter and trimeter lines and also by the incremental repetition of lines or (in this case) entire stanzas. "Black Jack Davey" moves forward by repeating itself with one small difference, and in this version of the ballad the difference is very small indeed: reiterating the young woman's acquiescence to Black Jack Davey's seduction, the verbs of the second stanza shift from the present imperative ("pull off them shoes") to the past indicative ("she pulled off them shoes").

This manner of stanzaic repetition is itself repeated throughout "Black Jack Davey," the accumulating two-stanza units giving the impression that the ballad's narrative moves forward only by circling back, telling the story twice. But near the song's conclusion this pattern is subtly altered. These two stanzas describe the young woman's unexpected refusal of her husband's final entreaty.

> Pull off, pull off them long blue gloves
> All made of the finest leather.
> Give to me your lily-white hand
> And we'll both go home together.
> We'll both go home together.

> Well, she pulled off them long blue gloves
> All made of the finest leather,
> Gave to him her lily-white hand
> And said good-bye forever,
> Bid farewell forever.

In the earlier pair of stanzas, we discover that the young woman's response to Black Jack Davey's command is *yes* when the present imperative shifts to the past indicative: the line "we'll ride off together" becomes "they rode off together." In this pair, we discover that the woman's response to her husband's command is *no*: the line "we'll go home together" becomes "said good-bye forever." The ballad's repeated instances of repetition make this pair of stanzas feel particularly surprising, but every such pair of stanzas enacts a discovery of difference through repetition. Having listened to "Black Jack Davey" once, we've already listened twice. And because twice is not enough, we listen again.

IX

SONG

"The words must of course determine the music," said Plato of what we've come to call lyric poems. Today, we no longer expect a lyric poem to be sung, though we continue to take pleasure in songs without expecting that their lyrics could necessarily be described as poems. The ear of someone who reads lots of poems might catch an elegant pentameter line in W. C. Handy—

I hate to see de ev'nin' sun go down

—or in the Rolling Stones—

I met a gin-soaked barroom queen in Memphis

—but our enjoyment of these songs is not contingent upon such recognitions, even if in the case of "Honky Tonk Woman" our pleasure does depend on the fact that, while the syncopated rhythm of the melody emphasizes the stressed syllables *gin* and

bar, the unstressed syllables *soaked* and *room*, with their prominently long vowel sounds, refuse to lie down quietly. The vitality
of great poems depends on such effects all the time, and precisely because we no longer imagine poems as songs, we expect
the language of a poem to marshal complicated rhythmic effects
on its own, unbolstered by a musical setting. Today, the *music* of
poetry could not be other than a metaphor.

"The great lyric age lasted while Campion made his own
music," said Pound, who lamented the fact that the ancient marriage of words and music had hit the rocks in the seventeenth
century. The Renaissance composer-poet Thomas Campion
stands apart for having set his own poems to music brilliantly;
he is as important to the history of English music as he is to
the history of English poetry. But the very word *lyric* tells a
more complicated story than Pound's remark suggests. Plato
described a sung poem not as *lyric* but as *melic*, and the word
lyric was not employed until after the third century BCE, when
the scholars of the Alexandrian library set out to preserve the
remaining poems of ancient Greek poets such as Sappho and
Anacreon. By this time, the musical settings of these poems
had been lost or disregarded, and, as the classicist Glenn Most
reminds us, the word *lyric* was coined to refer not to the experience of a sung poem but to the experience of a poem on the
page. From its first usages, the word commemorates the fraught
relationship of words and music, not their happy marriage.

Any of Campion's poetic contemporaries might have
expected their poems to be set to music; many of Campion's
musical contemporaries wrote beautiful settings of poems, as
the songs of the Renaissance composer John Dowland testify.
But like most of the lyrics set to music by Mick Jagger and Keith

Richards, the lyrics set to music by Dowland do not always sustain much interest outside the musical setting.

The **more** secure, the **more** the **stroke** we **feele**.

Campion offered this line in his "Observations in the Art of English Poesie" as what he called, without enthusiasm, a line of pure iambics: *ti **tum** ti **tum** ti **tum** ti **tum** ti **tum**.* Because all but one of the unstressed syllables are function words, and because the natural rhythm of the one multisyllabic word consorts easily with the ongoing metrical pattern, the line sounds straightforwardly iambic. The line "I met a gin-soaked barroom queen in Memphis" is more rhythmically complicated than that, and so is virtually every line that Campion wrote. The lines "Follow your Saint, follow with accents sweet" and "Follow thy faire sun, unhappy shadow" are both iambic pentameters, rich with echoing syllables, but the relationship of stressed to unstressed syllables is in each line unique.

Follow your **Saint**, **fol**low with **accents sweet**

Follow thy **faire sunne**, un**happy shad**dowe

Campion's great achievement lies not simply in the fact that he composed exquisite music for his own poems, but in the fact that his poems sustain the most subtle rhythmic effects on their own, effects that may challenge his musical settings.

Composing his *ayres*, as he called them, Campion often employed a six-line stanza (rhymed *ababcc*) that had long been a mainstay of the native tradition of English song, and typically he limited his ayres to two stanzas, making each stanza feel like one half of a strategically bivalve structure: like the two parts of Mark Strand's "Elevator," the two stanzas are the same but different, and the ayre refuses the resolution that a third iteration of the stanzaic pattern (much less a fourth or fifth) might provide. Campion covets this uneasy balance, for the life of his ayres inheres in the tension between their form (registered in the repetition of an identical stanza) and their structure (registered in the shape of the changing syntax that moves through the stanzas).

In itself, this tension is unremarkable. We've heard it in Shakespeare, in Moore, and in the anonymous lyric "Western Wind," which consists of three sentences that do not reinforce the formal symmetry of its single stanza (alternating tetrameters and trimeters rhymed *xaxa*). What happens if you add a second iteration of this same form?

> My life closed twice before its close—
> It yet remains to see
> If Immortality unveil
> A third event to me
>
> So huge, so hopeless to conceive
> As these that twice befell.
> Parting is all we know of heaven,
> And all we need of hell.

The two stanzas of this poem by Emily Dickinson share the form of "Western Wind," but while the two stanzas suggest that the poem will break into equal parts of four lines each, the syntax breaks into two unequal parts: when the first stanza concludes, the syntax of its sentence continues ("A third event to me / So huge, so hopeless"), making a six-line unit that is followed by the final epigrammatic two-line unit: "Parting is all we know of heaven, / And all we need of hell." As Dickinson suggests of her life, her poem closes twice, and without the resistance provided by the completed form of her first stanza, the poem's first sentence could not throw us so determinedly into the final two lines.

Campion's two-stanza ayres are designed to take full advantage of that resistance. The *ababcc* rhyme scheme of "When thou must home to shades of under ground" suggests that each stanza will break into a four-line unit (the *abab* quatrain) followed by a two-line unit (the couplet); this arrangement suggests in turn that something will be concluded at the end of the stanza, just as the final couplet of a Shakespearean sonnet makes us feel that something ought to be concluded. But as in Dickinson's poem, the ayre's first sentence does not end when the first stanza ends: this six-line adverbial clause is left hanging, its structural energy overriding the formal integrity of the couplet and throwing us into the second stanza.

> When thou must home to shades of under ground,
> And there ariv'd, a newe admired guest,
> The beauteous spirits do ingirt thee round
> White Iope, blith Helen, and the rest,
> To heare the stories of thy finisht love,
> From that smoothe toong whose musicke hell can move . . .

Then the first four lines of the second stanza complete the sentence.

> Then wilt thou speake of banqueting delights,
> Of masks and revels which sweete youth did make,
> Of Turnies and great challenges of knights,
> And all these triumphs for thy beauties sake.

Here, in the second stanza, the syntax has finally come to rest where the *abab* quatrain gives way to the final couplet, preparing us for the big finish. But when we turn to the couplet, the syntactical structure of the first ten lines of the poem (*When . . . then*) is repeated in two lines.

> When thou hast told these honours done to thee,
> Then tell, O tell, how thou didst murder me.

The ayre consists of two sentences that repeat the same structure, but this syntactical repetition is not synchronized with the formal repetition of the stanza. What's more, the final couplet's repetition of the poem's initial adverbial clause, reduced from six lines to one, divides the concluding couplet against itself, throwing much more weight on its revelatory second line: "Then tell, O tell, how thou didst murder me."

What happens to this animating tension when the poem is set to music? The fashion for the kind of songs Campion wrote, songs for a solo voice accompanied by a lute, was driven by the conviction that music should serve the text, making its sense intelligible rather than treating its syllables as opportunities for the sonic adventures that distinguished the polyphonic madrigal. Like many of his musical contemporaries, Campion was influenced by the Camerata, a group of Florentine musicians and theorists who championed a vocal line embodying the natural rhythms of syntax, and also by the Académie de Musique et de Poésie, whose members championed musical settings embodying the contrived rhythms of prosody. In my terms, the Italians wanted the musical setting of a poem to serve the poem's structure, while the French wanted the setting to serve the poem's form. So while the French tradition asks us to hear form at the expense of structure, the Italian asks us to hear structure at the expense of form: both traditions were motivated by the notion of serving the text, highlighting its intelligibility, but either tradition might be accused of diminishing the verbal life of the poem. Giulio Caccini, an influential composer associated with the Camerata, called polyphony a "laceration" of poetry, but poetry is already a laceration of itself, form and structure acting out tensions we experience as pleasure.

Campion did not use metaphors of violence, like laceration, to describe the proper relationship of text and music; on the contrary, like his French and Italian contemporaries, he spoke of his desire to "couple my Words and Notes lovingly together." At issue here is the nature of words. For if one imagines that the words of poems are at peace with one another, then it would be (as it were) loving to set them peacefully; however, if one understands that the words of a poem are constantly performing multiple tasks at once—the words broken into syllables that are commandeered by the poem's form, the words conjoined into clauses and phrases that are commandeered by the poem's structure—then it would be loving to set those words to music that may seem to resist the words.

Campion set his poems strophically; that is, each stanza is set to the same music, just as every stanza of "Black Jack Davey" is set to the same music. Listening to Bob Dylan sing this ballad, we first hear the setting of the lines in which the husband entreats his wife to come home with him.

> Pull off, pull off them long blue gloves
> All made of the finest leather.
> Give to me your lily-white hand
> And we'll both go home together.

Then we hear the lines describing the wife's refusal set to the same music.

> Well, she pulled off them long blue gloves
> All made of the finest leather,
> Gave to him her lily-white hand
> And said good-bye forever.

While the language of these two stanzas is almost identical until the fourth line, the musical setting of the two stanzas continues to be identical even as the language of the fourth line changes. The discovery of the wife's refusal is wrenching enough on the page, since the lyric's repetitions have led us to expect the line in the second stanza to be not "And said good-bye forever" but "And they went home together." The fact that the music doesn't change as the words change makes the discovery even more wrenching.

In Campion's strophic setting of "When thou must home to shades of under ground," the music repeats itself not only from stanza to stanza but within each stanza: the musical phrases setting the stanza's first five lines all begin with the same rhythm—three half notes followed by a dotted half note. And because the ayre is set in triple time, extra weight is thrown on the dotted half note, since it is always the downbeat of a new measure. As a result, the musical rhythm trumps the generally iambic rhythms of the lines: not *ti tum ti tum* ("When **thou** must **home**") but *ti* *ti ti tum* ("When thou must **home**"—"Then wilt thou **speak**"—"When thou hast **told**"). This rhythmic continuity makes the first five lines of each stanza feel wedded to one another, despite the fact that the first four lines are tied together by the *abab* rhyme scheme and consequently distinct from the fifth line, which is part of the concluding *cc* couplet.

What happens in the setting of the sixth line, which in the second stanza is so shockingly revelatory ("Then tell, O tell, how thou didst murder me")? After teaching us to expect a continuing rhythmic pattern (*ti ti ti tum*), Campion distinguishes the stanza's final line with a new rhythm (a half note rest followed by a half note, then two whole notes), a rhythm that throws the triple time off kilter by de-emphasizing the downbeat and making the song suddenly feel as if it were counted not in three but in two.

This manipulation of the musical meter, called a hemiola, may be most familiar from *West Side Story*, in which Leonard Bernstein's music makes us hear the dactylic line "I like to be in America" not as "**I** like to **be** in Amer**i**ca" but as "**I** like to **be** in Amer—**ic**—**a**." In Campion's song, the hemiola makes us hear the final line of the second stanza not as "Then tell, O tell," as the previous musical phrases had led us to expect, but as "Then **tell—O—tell**." Even on the page, that plangent "O" asked to be stressed, disrupting the more placid iambics of the previous line, and Campion's setting makes us hear the line's rhythm in exactly that way, creating a moment of dramatic tension perfectly suited to the way in which the poem's syntax throws us into the shocking conclusion of the second stanza: "Then tell, O tell, how thou didst murder me."

The same music cannot serve different words equally, however, and because both stanzas of the poem are set to the same music, the hemiola also occurs at the end of the first stanza, which (given the shape of its incomplete syntax) arrives at no conclusion whatsoever. But the way in which Campion's strophic settings alternately confirm or resist his syntax reinforces his decision to write poems that avoid an easy confluence of form and structure in the first place. It makes sense that a composer who was also a great poet would think this way; Campion was not setting prose sentences, after all, but a poem whose repetitive syntax is already at odds with its repetition of a stanza form. His poems are in tension with the music because they are productively in tension with themselves—which is why his poems remain gripping, independent of their musical settings, as many song lyrics do not.

Since the advent of recorded music, many of us have listened to songs we love over and over again; more recently, since the invention of the iPod, with its *repeat* function, many of us have done so obsessively—not because we can't remember the song's information as such, but because we enjoy the feeling of experiencing the song again, its musical and linguistic phrases moving forward in time. People who love poems, I've been arguing, similarly reread them not to acquire new knowledge but to reinhabit the enactment of what they already know, that enactment growing richer to the degree that they're seduced by the movement of the medium.

"Allow me to erect a straw man," says the musicologist Elizabeth Margulis in *On Repeat*, her study of musical repetition: "the notion that music is communicative, in the sense that it conveys information." The rhythmic and harmonic repetition crucial to musical structure, she continues, skewering her straw man, show that the transmission of information "cannot be music's primary function": the repetitive nature of music itself seduces us to repeat it. Syntactical, rhythmic, and phonological repetition, on which all poetic structure depends, suggests the same thing about poetry—even though the medium of poetry is inevitably communicative, as good for parking tickets as it is for poems. A poem's insight or information may be shockingly relevant, even after hundreds of years, but speaking metaphorically (because what we refer to easily as the *music* of poetry is in no strict sense musical), a permanently compelling poem is one that has already set itself to music.

X

TONE

What are poets talking about when they talk about tone? Ancient Greek rhetoricians used the word *tonos* (meaning, literally, a *tightening* or *stretching*, as a string on a lute might be stretched) to characterize the quality of an orator's performance of a speech; they were interested in describing the sounds produced by a particular human throat on a particular occasion. Predictably, our now more common sense of tone as the general quality of a written text, rather than the quality of a particular oratorical performance, began to prevail with the rise of print culture in the seventeenth century, and in the early years of the twentieth century the influential literary critic I. A. Richards defined poetic tone as a speaker's "attitude to his listener."

But it's important to remember that Richards uses the words *speaker* and *listener* metaphorically; he's talking about a written text, not an oratorical performance. Given that our sense of a poem's speaker is produced by the more fundamental characteristics of a poem's diction, syntax, and rhythm, how might we say that tone is produced similarly on the page? How are syllables, words, and phrases manipulated in order to produce the qualities we want to describe with the word *tone*?

Consider a simple sentence, three words, three syllables.

You said that

Depending on how we understand the syntax of this sentence, it might be a statement (*You said that*), a question (*You said that?*), or an exclamation (*You said that!*), and each one of these three sentences sounds a little different from the other two. One feels one's voice rising in the final syllable of the question, falling in the final syllable of the statement, and falling more dramatically in the final syllable of the exclamation.

Using the word *intonation* differently from the way musicians do, linguists would say that the statement, question, and exclamation are distinguished by three different intonations of the simple sentence. But the possibilities don't end there, for each of these three intonations will in turn sound different from itself, depending on which of the three syllables we emphasize; linguists refer to the emphasized syllable as the *tonic* syllable of an *intonational unit* (which is often but not necessarily a grammatical clause or phrase).

You *said that?*
You **said** *that?*
You said **that**?

In real life or on the stage, the context of an ongoing conversation might indicate these differences instantly, though often in real life we make mistakes about context, and sometimes we intentionally violate the decorum of a particular context; a child who asks *You **said** that?* at the wrong moment might be told sharply to *watch your tone*—a reprimand that deploys a visual metaphor to assert control over a sonic quality. How do you watch a tone?

The child might not know what to do if he were enjoined to *shift the emphasis from the second syllable of the question to the first*, but such adjustments are more precisely what we're responding to when we talk about the tone of a particular utterance: given the three available syntactical options (statement, question, exclamation), along with the three available placements of the tonic syllable (first, second, or third syllable emphasized), we could say that the sentence *you said that* might be uttered in nine different ways. A musical setting may emphasize the intonation of a particular line, as we've seen, but how exactly do poets make such discriminations clear on the page—as clear as they are when we're actually listening to a particular person at a particular time? Punctuation may of course distinguish a statement from a question, but how do we know that we're supposed to hear the question *You said that?* as ***You** said that?* and not as *You **said** that?*

The most obvious answer is typography, to which I've been resorting throughout this discussion; by highlighting a particular syllable or word, italic or bold type can signal the intonation of a particular word or phrase. Especially in his earlier poems, Frank Bidart does this with bracing accuracy.

> you   chip of the incommensurate
> closed world   *A n g e l*

The idiosyncratic use of punctuation, especially ungrammatical punctuation, can also score the intonation of a phrase, as we've seen in the poems of Emily Dickinson.

> Deals—One—imperial—Thunderbolt—

But Dickinson's procedures are almost impossible to imitate without seeming merely to be an imitator. And when deployed without Bidart's precision, typographical indications of rhythm may inadvertently highlight a poem's lack of intrinsic rhythmic vitality.

> Below the surface-stream, shallow and light,
> Of what we *say* we feel—below the stream,
> As light, of what we *think* we feel—there flows
> With noiseless current strong, obscure and deep,
> The central stream of what we feel indeed.

Here, the Victorian poet Matthew Arnold wants us to feel that, among the five stressed syllables in the line "As **light**, of **what** we **think** we **feel**—there **flows**," the greatest emphasis falls on *think*, making it the tonic syllable: "As light, of what we *think* we feel— there flows." A poem's tone may be ambiguous, and certainly part of a poem's allure may be due to our inability to describe its tone unequivocally. But Arnold's use of italics threatens to seem like compensation for an inability to control the intonation of his lines by poetic means, as if the strategic variation of the syntax within an ongoing metrical pattern were not enough.

Such control is precisely what we've heard Shakespeare muster in lines from his twelfth sonnet.

Borne on the **bier** with **white** and **bristly beard**

Four of these stressed syllables are linked by similar sounds (*borne, bier, bristly, beard*). But because *white* stands apart, we're liable to hear this syllable as the most emphatically emphasized of the five, giving the entire line a particular intonation: not *Borne on the **bier** with white and bristly beard* or *Borne on the bier with white and **bristly** beard* but

Borne on the bier with **white** and bristly beard.

Similarly, because four of the five stressed syllables in the following line share similar sounds (*loft, trees, see, leaves*)—

When **lofty trees** I **see bar**ren of **leaves**

—we're liable to hear the first syllable of *barren* as the most emphatically emphasized of the five, especially because this intrusion of an alien phoneme is reinforced by rhythmical variation. The line scans easily as an iambic pentameter, but the fourth iamb is flipped into a trochee (***barren***), throwing extra emphasis on the syllable that already stands apart, so we hear the line not as *When lofty **trees** I see barren of leaves* or as *When lofty trees I **see** barren of leaves* but as

When lofty trees I see **bar**ren of leaves.

Working together in this way, echo and metrical variation determine the precise intonation not only of these pentameters from Shakespeare but of pentameters by Keats—

Season of **mists** and **mel**low **fruit**ful**ness**

—in which *fruit* stands apart from *sea, mist, mel-*, and *-ness*, the extra emphasis on the syllable *fruit* enhanced by the way in which the three-syllable word *fruitfulness* makes the line's final stressed syllable fall away—

Season of mists and mellow **fruit**fulness

—and also of pentameters by Stevens—

On an **old shore**, the **vul**gar ocean **rolls**

—in which *vulgar* stands apart from *old, shore, ocean,* and *rolls*, the extra emphasis on the syllable *vul-* enhanced by the adjacency of the echoing syllables *old* and *shore* before the caesura preceding it.

On an old shore, the **vul**gar ocean rolls

Such synchronizations of echo and rhythm determine the intonation of innumerable metrical lines; there are as many possible variations of these procedures as there are lines to enact them.

How would a free-verse poem exert such control?

They taste good to her

This sentence from William Carlos Williams's "To a Poor Old Woman" is, like the sentence *you said that*, flat on the page. Linguists might say that there is no indication of the tonic syllable in this intonational unit; neither is there a metrical pattern that might be varied in order to throw emphasis on any particular syllable. Every poem chooses either explicitly or implicitly to do something at the expense of something else, however, and having relinquished the power of meter in this free-verse poem, Williams capitalizes on the power of line as a way to control the intonation of his syntax.

To a Poor Old Woman

munching a plum on
the street a paper bag
of them in her hand

They taste good to her
They taste good
to her. They taste
good to her

You can see it by
the way she gives herself
to the one half
sucked out in her hand

Following the first stanza's run-on syntax and enjambed lines, the second stanza's first line ("They taste good to her") feels whole and complete, a moment of stability. Subsequent lines animate this sentence by reintroducing enjambment to the poem's lineation, asking us to hear the sentence first as *they taste **good** to her* and then as *they **taste** good to her*. Each of these shifts in the placement of the tonic syllable adjusts the meaning of the sentence, but ultimately more provocative than the individual adjustments is the sequence of adjustments, which makes the poem feel purposefully thoughtful: it suggests that no one way of hearing the sentence will do complete justice to the rich experience of savoring the plum. "You can see it," says the poem's next line, but actually we've heard it, not seen it, the poem's lineation creating a sequence of rhythms that in turn generate what we call the poem's tone—the quietly rapt attentiveness it brings to even the most ordinary human pleasure.

Consider the lineation of Ellen Bryant Voigt's free-verse poem "Sleep," a poem whose unpunctuated syntax I examined earlier. This is not the way Voigt lineates her syntax.

> I flung myself into the car
> I drove like a fiend to the nearest store
> I asked unthinking for unfiltered Luckies
> oh brand of my girlhood
> I paid the price
> I took my prize to the car
> I slit the cellophane
> I tapped out one perfect white cylinder
> I brought to my face the smell of the barns

This, in contrast, is how Voigt actually lineates her syntax.

> I flung myself into the car I drove like a fiend
> to the nearest store I asked unthinkingly for unfiltered
>   Luckies oh
> brand of my girlhood I paid the price I took my prize to the
>   car I slit
> the cellophane I tapped out one perfect white cylinder I
>   brought to my face

the smell of the barns the fires cooking it golden brown smell
    of my father
my uncles my grandfather's tin of loose tobacco his packet of
    delicate paper
the deliberate way he rolled and licked and tapped and lit
    and drew in
and relished it the smell of the wild girls behind the gym
    the boys
in pickup trucks I sat in my car as the other cars crept by
I looked like a pervert it was perverse
a Lucky under my nose

What precisely do we mean if we say that these two lineations
of the poem's syntax have very different tones? Why, given that
the words are in each case identical, does the second arrangement sound fiercely self-aware, rueful yet comical, while the first
sounds self-satisfied?

Most of Voigt's clauses are linked paratactically, laid side
by side without subordination, and most of the clauses are
simply declarative as well. My imposed lineation preserves
the integrity of these clauses, resulting in a sequence of lines
beginning with the first person pronoun and a monosyllabic
verb (*I flung, I drove, I asked, I paid, I took, I slit, I tapped, I
brought*), and this fully synchronized repetition encourages us
to hear the tonic syllable in the same position in each line, producing a consistent rhythm: *I **flung** myself into the car, I **drove**
like a fiend, I **asked** unthinking.* As a result, the poem seems
like a record of considered thought (*I came, I saw, I conquered*),
rather than a volatile act of thinking. A similar synchroni-
zation of end-stopped lines and paratactic syntax in Donne's
"The Canonization"—

> For God's sake hold your tongue
> And let me love,
> Or chide my palsy,
> Or my gout

—similarly alters the tone, exasperation reduced to reason.

In contrast, Voigt's actual lineation of "Sleep" avoids any consistent alignment of syntax and line ("I slit / the cellophane"), violating the strong grammatical integrity of the clauses with enjambment and thereby disrupting the regular rhythm of the parallel syntax. At the same time, her lineation emphasizes the weaker grammatical links between the clauses by running them together ("I looked like a pervert it was perverse"), thereby creating variable rhythms within the lines.

It is not the lack of punctuation alone that produces this rhythmic vitality, for whether punctuated or not, each of Voigt's brief clauses is (like each of Donne's) easily understood, and the lack of punctuation accentuates the work that the syntax is already doing in relationship to the lines: the poem refuses to synchronize syntactical closure with linear closure, and these disjunctions between brief clauses and long lines deflate the already weak organizational power of the parataxis. The poem sounds like the work not of the reliable witness but of the raconteur, someone who doesn't realize "it was perverse" until the words "I looked like a pervert" provoke the insight. The tone is not predictably consistent, as it is in my relineated version of the poem, but rather consistently shifting, as it is in Williams's little poem.

Tone, says Voigt herself in what seems to me our finest available exploration of the topic, "is lodged primarily in the poem's nondiscursive elements, especially in its music. Music is meant here to include both the broad units of repetition, sentence structure, and lineation and the small units of syllable, vowel, and consonant." Voigt uses the metaphor of a poem's *music* carefully here, making it clear that poetic tone is produced not by musical but by linguistic devices—by the way in which the elements of the medium are arranged in order to produce what we recognize as tone, just as those elements are arranged to produce what we recognize as voice or image.

Contextual information may help us to determine the tone of a particular utterance, but unlike daily conversation, lyric poems are often short on context, and some have none at all. Because tone, however equivocal, may be deduced most reliably from the sonic properties of the language, we may be guided by tone long before we've had a chance to determine what the poem is about; rereading a poem, we may remain captivated by its tone long after we've understood the poem so well we know it by heart.

XI ❧

PROSE

Lyric, epic, dramatic: this tripartite division has been a commonplace in western aesthetics since the eighteenth century, and while ancient precedents were invoked to justify it, Plato and Aristotle in fact had almost nothing to say about the poetry they called *melic* rather than *lyric*. The word *lyric,* as I've mentioned, was not coined until after the third century BCE, when the librarians of Alexandria began collecting the remaining fragments of Pindar, Sappho, and Anacreon. "Imagine," says the classicist W. R. Johnson, "all of English literature from Chaucer to Tennyson, long circulated in manuscripts indifferent and bad, suddenly dumped helter-skelter in your lap. The task that confronted the Alexandrian scholar-librarians was herculean."

Today there is of course an enormous body of lyric poems in English to look back on, from before Chaucer to after Tennyson, and if our long-term investment in the epic has seemed to dwindle, it's because the narrative energies of the epic poem have since the eighteenth century been subsumed by the novel.

With the rise of the novel's prestige, poetry became increasingly synonymous with lyric poetry, and tensions between narrative and lyric modes came to seem increasingly fraught. Novelists told stories; poets offered fleeting glimpses. At the same time, poets coveted the worldliness that seemed to come naturally to prose writers, and prose writers coveted the interiority that had come to seem the special province of the lyric. Not coincidentally, the prose-poem's equivocal status became increasingly pressing, and in certain circumstances the words *lyric* and *narrative* could each describe writing that was not to be admired. This continues to be the case even today.

Yet the medium from which both poems and prose are made is the same medium: one can as easily describe the diction, syntax, rhythm, or tone of a prose narrative as of a lyric poem, as my brief description of Donne's prose suggests. I've been emphasizing that any lyric poem is forged from these primary elements, just as a painting is forged from a manipulation of the primary colors; but what might be the difference between a passage of prose we're tempted to call lyrical and a passage of prose that actually inhabits a lyric structure?

Consider a passage from Ernest Hemingway's *In Our Time* ("senta" is an Italian command, meaning "listen").

> Rinaldi lay still in the sun breathing with difficulty. "You and me we've made a separate peace. Senta. Senta Rinaldi." Nick turned his head carefully and looked at Rinaldi. Stretcher bearers would be along any time now. It was going well. Things were getting forward in the town. Up the street were other dead. Two Austrian dead lay in the rubble in the shade of the house. The pink wall of the house opposite

had fallen out from the roof, and an iron bed-
stead hung twisted toward the street. Nick looked
straight ahead brilliantly. Rinaldi, big backed, his
equipment sprawling, lay face downward against
the wall. The day was very hot. The sun shone on
his face. His face was sweaty and dirty. He had been
hit in the spine.

Here, I've arranged Hemingway's sentences backwards: because
the syntax is exclusively paratactic, the passage makes as much
sense as when arranged forwards. But like my rearranged versions of "Western Wind" or "No Possum, No Sop, No Taters,"
this rearranged passage has a very different effect, despite the
fact that its information is unchanged. Observation follows
observation, and we are left to deduce whatever elements of
causation determine their order—or, more provocatively, we
are left to feel that the order has determined whatever sense of
causation we've deduced.

Arranged forwards or backwards, this passage does not foreground the construction of narrative time, but especially when
arranged backwards, its sentences build a structure familiar
from lyric poems because we do not begin with foundational
information ("He had been hit in the spine") that is then elab-
orated upon, *spine* leading by contiguity to *face* and then to *sun*.
Instead, the same information appears not as foundation but as
discovery, for after we move through the same associative chain
in reverse (*sun, face, spine*), the shift from the simple past ("His
face was sweaty") to the past perfect ("He had been hit in the
spine") feels revelatory. If these sentences were lineated as complete syntactical units—

The **day** was **very hot**.
The **sun shone** on his **face**.
His **face** was **sweat**y and **dirt**y.
He had been **hit** in the **spine**.

—we'd feel that the additional function words required to enact the shift to the past perfect (*had been*) also enact a rhythmic shift, a movement from three-beat lines to a two-beat line larded with extra unstressed syllables. If these sentences were lineated in the order in which they actually appear—

He had been hit in the spine.
His face was sweaty and dirty.
The sun shone on his face.
The day was very hot.

—their tone would recall the tone of my relineation of Voigt's "Sleep," the rhythm of the parallel syntax settling into a relentless predictability. While the forward version of this passage does reach for the rich verbal texture we associate with lyric poems, the backward version harnesses the revelatory power of lyric structure.

"Karintha," from Jean Toomer's *Cane*, harnesses that power self-consciously. This hybrid construction opens with a quatrain that is subsequently repeated between short passages of prose. This refrain also repeats itself internally.

Her skin is like dusk on the eastern horizon,
O cant you see it, O cant you see it,
Her skin is like dusk on the eastern horizon
. . . When the sun goes down.

We've seen, reading Wyatt, that a refrain embodies the wish that something might stay the same while also reinvigorating our knowledge that everything will change: "Her skin is like dusk . . . Her skin is like dusk." Following the first iteration of this refrain is a brief prose narrative describing the preternaturally seductive Karintha as a child: predictably, hypotactic syntax dominates the narrative.

> At dusk, during the hush just after the sawmill had closed down, and before any of the women had started their supper-getting-ready songs, her voice, high-pitched, shrill, would put one's ears to itching.

But as "Karintha" moves forward, the lyric impulse of the refrain enters the syntax of the prose. After the second iteration of the refrain comes a brief prose passage in the present tense: Karintha has grown up, and the sentences shift from hypotaxis to parataxis.

> Karintha is a woman. Young men run stills to make her money. Young men go to the big cities and run on the road. Young men go away to college. They all want to bring her money.

The final prose section shifts from the present to the future tense ("They will bring her money; they will die not having found it out"), asserting that the future will be exactly like the present. And while the final iteration of the refrain returns us to the place we've always been ("Her skin is like dusk on the eastern horizon"), the figure "like dusk" also suggests the opposite of stasis, and one has to wonder if the stasis "Karintha" covets is either possible or desirable.

Toomer's *Cane* and Hemingway's *In Our Time* stand among several important books, published in the 1920s, that were constructed from a mixture of different kinds of writing, simultaneously disaggregated and whole. Another was of course James Joyce's *Ulysses*, and while Toomer aspired to the condition of lyric, Joyce had epic ambitions: the eighteen episodes of *Ulysses* are based on eighteen episodes in Homer's *Odyssey*. But while these correspondences helped to determine Joyce's narrative, they more importantly offered Joyce a logic that determined the book's wildly disparate stylistic experiments. On the one hand, *Ulysses* acts like an unrelentingly intense exploration of the lives of its characters, but on the other hand, it acts like an elaborately designed verbal confection, its dazzling linguistic surface sometimes threatening to occlude the very illusion of life that it so vividly creates.

In itself, this tension is hardly unique; like poems, novels are made of words. But the strenuousness with which Joyce inhabits this tension often makes the experience of reading *Ulysses* feel like the experience of reading a poem, since poems exist in order to foreground such tensions to a degree that other kinds of verbal contraptions, which traffic in other kinds of knowledge, may not. If *Ulysses* deserves in this regard to be called lyrical, however, it inhabits a lyric structure only sporadically—though it does so at junctures so crucial that the book's epic ambitions are challenged.

In the episode that corresponds to Odysseus's battle with the gigantic one-eyed Cyclops, Joyce's protagonist, Leopold Bloom, is attacked by a myopically nationalistic Irishman referred to as the Citizen. The language of this episode is itself gigantic and shortsighted: this is a description of a man sitting in the pub at which the altercation takes place.

> The figure seated on a large boulder at the foot of a round tower was that of a broadshouldered deep-chested stronglimbed frankeyed redhaired freely-freckled shaggybearded widemouthed largenosed longheaded deepvoiced barekneed brawnyhanded hairylegged ruddyfaced sinewyarmed hero.

This playfulness is purposeful. At the climax of this episode, Bloom responds to the Citizen's openly anti-Semitic taunts with "Christ was a jew like me," enraging the Citizen. But Bloom is playing a role here, allowing himself to be seen shortsightedly. For while Bloom's father Rudolph was born a Hungarian Jew, Rudolph converted to Protestantism before Bloom was born; Bloom's mother was an Irish Catholic named Ellen Higgins, and Bloom himself was baptized first as a Protestant and later as a Catholic, before he married his wife Molly.

All the characters in *Ulysses* assume that Bloom is Jewish, and by distracting us from narrative information with the play of language, Joyce allows us initially to make the same assumption. Bloom doesn't consider himself a Jew, but he stands up for righteousness by embracing the identity conferred on him by his culture: later in the day, he describes his standoff with the Citizen this way: "[I] told him his God, I mean Christ, was a jew too and all his family like me though in reality I'm not." The Citizen's nationalism would perpetuate anti-Semitism, Joyce suggests, even if there were, in reality, no Irish Jews. The prejudice is perpetuated by the language, and the language of *Ulysses* seems to have a life of its own, larger than any individual who happens to harness it, larger than any individual whom it names.

By saying so, I may seem to have come a long way from describing the syntax of lyric poems, but inasmuch as poems by Shakespeare or Stevens have come a long way from Homer, the steps I've taken are small. In the third century BCE the Alexandrian poet-librarian Callimachus responded impatiently to readers who expected him to emulate Homer's epic grandeur—

> The malignant gnomes who write reviews in Rhodes
> are muttering about my poetry again

—and then defended himself with unexpected tenderness.

> Nightingales are honey-pale
> and small poems are sweet.

Callimachus, whom I quote in the translation by Stanley Lombardo and Diane Rayor, wanted to liberate the newly named genre of the lyric from the pressures of epic prestige, and his own poems became crucial for the later Latin poets, most prominently Horace and Propertius, who repeated Callimachus's defense of dilatory songs of love over violent narratives of war. When Campion proposes in one of his songs that "If all would lead their lives in love like me, / Then bloodie swords and armour should not be," he is expressing his inheritance of this preference for lyric over epic.

So is the pacifist Bloom when, defying the anti-Semitic Citizen, he champions "love" against "force, hatred, history, all that." *Ulysses* concludes not with an Odyssean slaying of the suitors but with the most rapturous hymn to sexual love in our language, a hymn in which the syntax is almost relentlessly paratactic.

> and then I asked him with my eyes to ask again
> yes and then he asked me would I yes to say yes my
> mountain flower and first I put my arms around
> him yes and drew him down to me so he could feel
> my breasts all perfume yes and his heart was going
> like mad and yes I said yes I will Yes.

But if love vanquishes epic violence in *Ulysses*, it is not without great struggle. In the novel's penultimate episode, Bloom sits alone in his house, surveying its contents as if it were the contents of his mind. He opens the drawers of his desk. He picks up an envelope containing his father's suicide note, but does not open it. As he has done many times before, he recites snippets of the note by heart.

> Tomorrow will be a week that I received . . . . it is
> no use Leopold to be . . . . with your dear mother . . .
> that is not more to stand . . . to her . . . all for me is
> out . . . be kind to Athos, Leopold . . . . my dear
> son . . . always . . . of me . . . *das Herz . . . Gott . . .*
> *dein . . .*

Das Herz, Gott, dein: the heart, God, yours. Athos: the dog. Bloom is not reciting a lyric poem, but he is giving himself over to the process of lyric knowledge. The discovery he willingly repeats here, the discovery of his father's death, is not in itself pleasurable; the act of repetition induces comfort. Having survived one long day, Bloom needs to reimagine the next long day, a day that will not be so very different. "That which is repeated has been—otherwise it could not be repeated," writes Kierkegaard in *Repetition*, "but the very fact that it has been makes the repetition into something new."

It's in this sense, as I began this book by proposing, that the pleasure of lyric knowledge is not something we necessarily experience only by reading poems. Prose may be the vehicle. Setting the dinner table may become the vehicle when the act of arranging the silverware, napkins, and plates becomes as gratifying as the act of eating. But poems are a more reliable vehicle because they exist not necessarily to be useful (as vessels for information or for food), but to allow us to take pleasure in repeatable actions that may seem, not only on the worst of days but on the best of days, to constitute our uselessness. Everybody needs to eat; nobody needs to read poems, though at certain moments the sustenance provided by the act of reading a poem may feel as necessary as food.

XII

POETRY

Imagine that poems were easy to write. Looking inward or outward, poets would say what they feel and describe what they see. They would produce as many poems as there are moments of insight or observation to be had, and each of these poems would be as obviously pertinent to our lives, day by day, minute by minute, as parking tickets or recipes for chocolate cake. Rarely would we bother to read anyone's poems but our own, rarely would we read a poem twice; we'd write a new poem instead.

But of course poems are not just difficult but often impossible to write, especially when insight and observation abound; every poet knows how it feels to write badly, once having written well. Although a poem may well be provoked by a moment of insight or observation, a poem is a record of its maker's passionate relationship with the medium, and while that relationship is fraught, like any such relationship, the record is permanently available. A poem is an invitation to return to the site of love.

The poet's medium, as I've emphasized, consists not only

of the diction, syntax, rhythms, and figures of the language in which a poet happens to write. Because the effect of a particular poem depends on the arrangement of these fundamental elements in relationship to one another, the medium also consists of the ways in which these elements have been arranged in previous poems; in this sense, the knowledge we derive from a lyric is inevitably a repetition of what we already know, even if we're encountering a poem for the first time. "For me the initial delight is in the surprise of remembering something I didn't know I knew," said Robert Frost of his experience of encountering a great poem: "I am in a place, a situation, as if I had materialized from cloud or risen out of the ground." Anyone might write something that feels like a lyric poem, that makes its readers feel what Frost describes, but we wouldn't recognize that utterance as a lyric unless we'd first read one elsewhere.

How then did poetry in English begin? In his eighth-century *Ecclesiastical History of the English People*, the Venerable Bede tells the story of Cædmon, who late in his life joined a monastery in the north of England. Sometimes at a feast, says Bede, the monks would sing for one another, but when Cædmon "saw the harp approaching him, he would rise up in the middle of the feasting, go out, and return home." Cædmon was no singer, no poet, though he liked a good feast. *Nonnumquam in convivio*, writes Bede in the original Latin, *sometimes at a feast*. When Bede's history was translated into Old English in the ninth century, before the language contained any Latinate words, the word *convivio* was rendered as *gebeorscipe*, which means *beer-ship* or *drinking of beer together*.

One night, Cædmon had a dream in which he was again enjoined to sing something. "What must I sing?" he asked. The dream instructed him to sing of the creation of all things, which

Cædmon then did without hesitation. He remembered the poem when he awoke, and for the rest of his life he was renowned for his ability to compose beautiful poems on demand, a new poem for every new day. "He did not learn the art of poetry from men nor through a man," says Bede, "but he received the gift of song freely by the grace of God."

Here is my very loose translation of the Old English poem we've come to call "Cædmon's Hymn." To make it sound like a free-verse poem in modern English, I've introduced some Latinate diction, reorganized the syntax, consolidating its many repetitions, and altered the lineation better to serve this syntax and diction.

> Now must we praise the guardian of heaven,
> His power and his understanding,
> Holy creator, father of glory, eternal lord—
> How he originated every wondrous thing.
> First he made heaven as a roof
> For earth's children.
> Then he created earth,
> The lord almighty adorned the earth for mankind.

Even if Cædmon learned nothing from men, as Bede says, what did he learn from his medium? While "Cædmon's Hymn" was composed in the English spoken in the north of England in Bede's time, its syntax organized in the four-beat alliterative line typical of Old English poems, the hymn was first written down as Latin prose; offering his translation, Bede cautions that he provides the sense but not the order of the original words. Today, we do possess Old English versions of "Cædmon's Hymn," but they were either added to Bede's Latin text or included in Old

English translations of Bede, the translations that rendered *convivio* as *drinking of beer together*. In Bede's history, "Cædmon's Hymn" is a poem created out of nothing, but on the page "Cædmon's Hymn" is a poem derived from precedent, the result of one medium giving way to another, just as my translation of the poem is the result of one medium giving way to another.

Early readers of "Cædmon's Hymn" would have known about one true act of creation *ex nihilo*, out of nothing: "In the beginning God created the heaven and the earth," begins the book of Genesis. Advertising the fact that it is made out of something, "Cædmon's Hymn" repeats this familiar biblical language: God "first created the heavens as a roof for the children of men and then . . . created the earth," says the poem in Bede's prose version. We've seen that acts of repetition become acts of transformation, however, and while Bede's version of "Cædmon's Hymn" says that God created *caelum* as a roof, using the Latin word meaning both heaven and sky, the Old English versions of the poem use the Germanic word *heofon*, from which we derive our modern English word *heaven*. In Germanic English, but not in Latin, what exists in *heaven* has been *heaved* there from the earth below. Even if Cædmon were divinely inspired, the medium of the English language made his poem.

These opening lines of Frank Bidart's "Genesis 1–2:4" were made near the end of the twentieth century.

In the beginning, God made HEAVEN and EARTH.

The earth without form was waste.

DARKNESS was the face of the deep.
His spirit was the wind brooding over the waters.

Every line of this poem is familiar, but no line is exactly like any previous English translation of Genesis: "In the bigynnyng God made of nouyt heuene and erthe" (Wycliffe); "In the begynnynge God created heaven and erth" (Tyndale); "In the beginning God created the heaven and the earth" (King James). Like Cædmon, Bidart has made something out of something, but for Bidart, the *something* from which he is making his poem has been enriched by an additional thousand years of usage; the medium of his poem includes not only the diction and syntax of the developing English language but the particular ways in which that diction and syntax have been arranged by previous makers into particular sentences. So while Bidart's "Genesis 1–2:4" may seem like a special case, a poem that only repeats existing language, just as Mark Strand's "Elevator" may seem uniquely like a poem that only repeats itself, "Genesis 1–2:4" in fact reminds us that all poems are made of words that come trailing the glories of prior usages. To avoid those usages is to distance oneself from the medium, to step away from the site of love.

"I made it out of a mouthful of air," says W. B. Yeats in a moment of lyric extravagance. "But the medium of this is language," says the philosopher Theodor Adorno. Precisely because poems are made of language, which is social, distinctive to no one, a poem never belongs to the poet alone. The poet's act of submitting himself to the stubborn reality of the medium is paradoxically indistinguishable from the poet's act of self-expression, says Adorno: "This is why the lyric reveals itself to be most deeply grounded in society when it does not chime in with society, when it communicates nothing, when, instead, the subject whose expression is successful reaches an accord with language itself, with the inherent tendency of the language."

Mostly, poets experience the failure to achieve this perfect accord with their medium, but in a great poem, what is social seems personal, what is derived from precedent feels distinctive, made in the moment. How does this happen?

The majority of lyric poems I've described in this book are written in the present tense. Cædmon: "Now must we praise." Shakespeare: "When lofty trees I see." Dickinson: "He fumbles at your Soul." This selection is representative of lyric poems at large, which are written overwhelmingly in the present tense—so much so that we take for granted how peculiar the lyric's inhabitation of the simple present actually sounds. When Yeats begins "Among School Children" by saying "I walk through the long schoolroom," he doesn't sound like a speaker of the English language: who actually talks that way, describing what he's doing in the simple present, rather than in the present progressive ("I'm walking through the long schoolroom")? The lyric present is an artifice that has come to seem natural; it signals that the utterance we're about to experience wants to seem unprecedented, happening now.

But to sustain that impression a poem needs more than a signal: how does any poem, even a poem recounting past events, sustain the visceral impression that it's happening now? Samuel Taylor Coleridge's "Kubla Khan" is conspicuously a past-tense lyric; it is also a lyric that, like "Cædmon's Hymn," came to its author in a dream.

> In Xanadu did Kubla Khan
> A stately pleasure-dome decree:
> Where Alph, the sacred river, ran
> Through caverns measureless to man
>   Down to a sunless sea.

So twice five miles of fertile ground
With walls and towers were girdled round:
And there were gardens bright with sinuous rills
Where blossomed many an incense-bearing tree;
And here were forests ancient as the hills,
Enfolding sunny spots of greenery.

The dream provoking these lines fulfilled a lyric wish for immediacy: "the images rose up before him as things," said Coleridge,
speaking of himself in the third person. But like "Cædmon's
Hymn," "Kubla Khan" is made from the medium Coleridge
shared with other people: its opening lines are adapted from
a seventeenth-century travel narrative ("In Xamdu did Cublai
Can build a stately . . . house of Pleasure"), and, as John Livingston Lowes demonstrated in the magisterial *Road to Xanadu*,
virtually every word of "Kubla Khan" may be traced to
Coleridge's compulsive reading of such narratives.

Nor does the poem suppress this indebtedness, for as "Kubla
Khan" unfolds, its drama inheres not in its story of the creation
of the pleasure dome, raised beside the ominously violent river
Alph, but in the ongoing creative act of the poet's negotiation
with his medium.

A damsel with a dulcimer
In a vision once I saw:
It was an Abyssinian maid,
And on her dulcimer she played,
Singing of Mount Abora.
Could I revive within me
Her symphony and song,
To such a deep delight 'twould win me,

> That with music loud and long,
> I would build that dome in air,
> That sunny dome! those caves of ice!

Here, when Coleridge shifts abruptly from the account of Khan's story in the past tense ("In Xanadu did Kubla Khan / A stately pleasure-dome decree") to this first-person account of an apparently unrelated narrative ("A damsel with a dulcimer / In a vision once I saw"), the simple past gives way first to the subjunctive—

> Could I revive within me
> Her symphony and song

—then to the conditional.

> I would build that dome in air,
> That sunny dome! those caves of ice!

Anyone privy to this poetic act of creation would cry "Beware! / His flashing eyes, his floating hair," the pronoun now referring not to the magisterial Khan but to the maker of the poem, the conditional giving way to the present imperative—

> Weave a circle round him thrice,
> And close your eyes with holy dread

—before reverting to the past.

> For he on honey-dew hath fed,
> And drunk the milk of Paradise.

Coleridge figures his poem as a making of something out of next-to-nothing, honey-dew transfigured into language, but the figure itself is extruded from the poem's struggle to make something out of something, thereby making us feel intimate with the act of making: could the poet reanimate the song of the damsel, he would translate his vision of the pleasure dome into the language of the very poem we're reading now.

Infamously, Coleridge maintained that "a person on business from Porlock" interrupted the writing of "Kubla Khan," causing the poem to remain unfinished; the language of social interaction invaded the private space of lyric reverie. But the poem suggests that the construction of that space depends on social interaction: the poet's reverie is contingent upon his recollection of the damsel's song, and, more precisely, as Coleridge's deployment of borrowed language insists, the poem itself is forged from the linguistic medium shared by dreaming poets and persons from Porlock alike. The vision of the damsel with a dulcimer interrupts the story of what happened in Xanadu, and the resulting shifts in the tense and mood of the poem's verbs direct our attention to the act of articulating what happened, the act of coming to know, which in a lyric poem is always happening now.

From the beginning of this book, I've emphasized the importance of such shifting. Our experience of a lyric is determined not simply by its diction, syntax, figuration, or rhythm, but by the way the poem orders its movement between Latinate and Germanic diction—

> than the sea when it proffers flattery in exchange
>   for hemp,
> rye, flax, horses, platinum, timber and fur

—or between paratactic and hypotactic syntax—

> Take you a course, get you a place,
> Observe his honour, or his grace,
> Or the King's real, or his stamped face
>   Contemplate, what you will, approve,
> So you will let me love

—or between discontinuous figures—

> A scattered chapter, livid hieroglyph,
> The portent wound in corridors of shells

—or between regular and irregular rhythms—

> Though the night was made for loving,
>   And the day returns too soon,
> Yet we'll go no more a roving
>   By the light of the moon

—or between varying densities of echo.

> And summer's green all girded up in sheaves
> Borne on the bier with white and bristly beard

I've also shown that even a poem synchronizing its repetitions of diction, syntax, figure, rhythm, and echo may nonetheless feel like an unstable act of becoming, one thing following another in a way that feels simultaneously unpredictable and inevitable; I've shown how this seductively erratic movement of language may cause us to reach for the metaphors of poetic voice or tone. The lyric poem offers not extractable knowledge but what feels like an act of thinking that transpires in the time it takes to read the poem. I say *what feels like* an act of thinking because, as the word *immediacy* reminds us, that act is produced through a poet's devotedly meticulous relationship with the *medium*; we have no access to the poet's mind. If we did, we wouldn't feel compelled to read poems, much less read them again. We would experience our pleasure immediately, without the intervention of a medium.

Any reader who takes pleasure in poems also knows what it feels like to be left cold, just as every poet knows how it feels to fail. Especially when we're in love, repetition may threaten to degenerate from rapture to routine; the feelings we point to with a word like *rapture* wouldn't feel authentic if they weren't so poignantly contingent, and, as Freud suggests repeatedly, the adult psyche may fall too easily into an unproductive repetition of what matters to it most. This is why poets, like lovers, must continually reanimate ways of doing the same thing over again, no matter how enduring the achievement of previous poems. My initial question—*how did poetry in English begin?*—is asked by every new poem forged from the medium. Every poet is a beginner. All poets are Cædmon.

"I have seen it over and over, the same sea, the same," laments Elizabeth Bishop in "At the Fishhouses," the water swinging icily "above the stones and then the world"—as if the stultifying sameness of the water were a psychic condition that could swallow us, turning us all into stones. But then Bishop finds a way not to transform the dark water (that's after all not possible) but to transform the repeated experience of it, so that the water no longer functions as a mirror for misery: rather than dipping her hand into the water, rather than tasting it, she wonders what such experience of water would be like—she makes a metaphor.

> It is like what we imagine knowledge to be:
> dark, salt, clear, moving, utterly free,
> drawn from the cold hard mouth
> of the world, derived from the rocky breasts
> forever, flowing and drawn, and since
> our knowledge is historical, flowing, and flown.

What does it mean to say that knowledge is *free* but forever *derived*? How could knowledge be *flowing*, happening in the moment of its discovery, but at the same time *flown*, always having existed prior to the moment of discovery, waiting to happen again? Every lyric poem answers these questions, not with what it says but with its transformative act of saying. This knowledge, lyric knowledge, comes to us in language that is flowing because it has flown.

ACKNOWLEDGMENTS

The shape of this book first became clear to me about ten years ago, and over the past decade, I've formulated versions of its observations in a variety of essays and reviews. I'm grateful to the editors of the following magazines and books for permission to repurpose sentences and paragraphs that first appeared in their pages: *The Nation, Poetry, Raritan, The Yale Review, The Writer's Chronicle*, and *John Donne in Context*.

Friends, colleagues, and students at the University of Rochester, the Warren Wilson MFA Program for Writers, the Bread Loaf Writers' Conference, and the Bogliasco Foundation have been equally supportive, and for various kinds of insight and advice I'm especially indebted to Debra Allbery, Matthew Bailey-Shea, Michael Collier, Jeff Dolven, Morris Eaves, Deborah Fox, Louise Glück, Jennifer Grotz, Thomas Hahn, Sally Keith, John Palattella, Donald Revell, Martha Rhodes, Michael Schoenfeldt, Susan Uselmann, and Ellen Bryant Voigt.

Matthew Bevis, Kenneth Gross, Langdon Hammer, and Russ McDonald read drafts of the entire book, offering crucial suggestions. Joanna Scott, my first reader, my last reader, participated in the making of every one of its sentences. I finish this book with a lifetime's worth of gratitude and love.

FURTHER READING

Diction

The most engaging history of the English language that I know is Seth Lerer's recent *Inventing English*; a more systematic account may be found in Albert Baugh's venerable *A History of the English Language*. In contrast to the more thesis-driven work of Owen Barfield or Donald Davie, Robert Pinsky's *The Sounds of Poetry* contains brief but provocative descriptions of the inevitably mongrel nature of English diction; Marie Borroff's *Language and the Poet* offers focused accounts of that diction in modern poems. The ways in which translation highlights questions of English diction are explored in John Hollander's "Versions, Interpretations, and Performances."

Syntax

While there exist many guides to English grammar and syntax, Charles Fries's *The Structure of English* is refreshingly descriptive, eschewing all jargon. With some degree of polemical fervor, the mid-twentieth-century poet-critics William Empson and Donald Davie, along with critic William Baker, pushed syntax to the forefront of our thinking about poems: a poet writing today will want to begin with Ellen Bryant Voigt's indispensable *The Art of Syntax*. Inasmuch as the effect of a poem's lineation cannot be described without attention to a poem's syntax, my own *The Art of the Poetic Line* may also be helpful.

Voice

Building on influential remarks by modern poets (especially T. S. Eliot and Robert Frost), Cleanth Brooks and Robert Penn Warren's influential teaching anthology, *Understanding Poetry*, made "voice" an almost inevitable aspect of the analysis of English-language poetry. A critique of this apparent inevitability may be found in Charles Bernstein's "Writing and Method," in *Content's Dream,* and, more concertedly, in Jonathan Culler's *Theory of the Lyric*. In *Poetry and the Fate of the Senses* Susan Stewart lays groundwork for a rehabilitation of the notion of poetic voice.

Figure

The novelist Christine Brooke-Rose's *A Grammar of Metaphor* remains as dazzling as it seemed half a century ago. So does William Empson's *Seven Types of Ambiguity*. Indispensable for thinking about the work of figuration in any human utterance is George Lakoff and Mark Johnson's *Metaphors We Live By*. And far more usefully wide-ranging than its modest title suggests, Stephen Booth's *An Essay on Shakespeare's Sonnets* offers (among other things) instructively lucid accounts of the work of figuration in poems. More interested in the ways poets and critics have understood figuration is Denis Donoghue's *Metaphor*.

Rhythm

While almost any handbook to English poetry will discuss rhythm and meter, even the best are often marred by polemic (free-verse poems are inferior to metered poems or vice versa) or by knee-jerk assumptions about form and content (free-verse poems are suspicious of order, metered poems embrace it). Wonderfully free of these myopias is Derek Attridge's *Poetic Rhythm: An Introduction*; also Charles Hartman's *Free Verse*. John Thompson's *The Founding of English Metre* is, like Steven Booth's book, far more wide-ranging in its implications than its title suggests. A good introduction to Old English prosody may be found in Donald Scragg's "The Nature of Old English Verse."

Echo

Hugh Kenner's "Rhyme: An Unfinished Monograph" offers surprising observations about the species of echo we call rhyme, as does Susan Stewart's *The Poet's Freedom*; Robert Pinsky's *The Sounds of Poetry* is especially good at describing rhyme as one of many ways in which words may sound like one another. John Hollander's *The Figure of Echo* explores both physical and metaphorical versions of echo. And probably no one is better at describing the way poems echo other poems than Christopher Ricks. On nonsense, see Stewart's *Nonsense*.

Image

Like our conceptions of the poetic voice, our commonplace notions of the poetic image congealed around a variety of influential remarks made by modern poets, especially Ezra Pound and T. S. Eliot. Witheringly critical of those notions is William Empson's "Rhythm and Imagery in English Poetry," in *Argufying*, and P. N. Furbank's *Reflections on the Word "Image"*; one needn't agree with their critiques to benefit from their analyses. More recent considerations of the relationship of visual, verbal, and mental images may be found in W.T.J. Mitchell's *Iconology* and Elaine Scarry's *Dreaming by the Book*.

Repetition

Unless it's Plato or St. Augustine, the place where all ladders start must be either Sigmund Freud's "Remembering, Repeating, and Working Through" or Søren Kierkegaard's *Repetition*, both of which make insight feel like drama. Gertrude Stein's "Portraits and Repetition," in *Lectures in America*, is highly provocative, as is Elizabeth Margulis's *On Repeat*, though it underestimates the power of repetition in poems. More to the point is John Hollander's "Breaking into Song: Some Notes on Refrain," in *Melodious Guile*. In *A Handlist of Rhetorical Terms* Richard Lanham describes the various schemes of repetition (anaphora, chiasmus, etc.) named by ancient rhetoricians.

Song

While many poets have written about the "music" of poetry (perhaps most famously T. S. Eliot), few have anything pertinent to say about music as such, consequently muddying our sense of what the "music" of poetry might be. In contrast, James Winn's *Unsuspected Eloquence: A History of the Relations between Poetry and Music* describes music as intimately as it describes poems, as does Elise Jorgens's *The Well-Tun'd Word: Musical Interpretations of English Poetry, 1597–1651*. Throughout the brilliant *Counter-Statement*, Kenneth Burke's dynamically temporal sense of poetic form is derived from his experience as a musician.

Tone

The most approachable discussion of tone in the linguistic sense is, in my experience, Paul Tench's *The Intonation Systems of English*. In "Intonation and the Conventions of Free Verse" Natalie Gerber adapts the terms of linguistics to a supple discussion of tone in free-verse poems. Less technical but bracingly clarifying is Ellen Bryant Voigt's "On Tone," in *The Flexible Lyric,* which is equally good at diagnosing the problems with earlier discussions of poetic tone and at laying the groundwork for a truly meaningful discussion.

Prose

Wallace Stevens called Ernest Hemingway "the most significant of living poets." John Donne's or Marianne Moore's prose would command our attention if they had written no poems. Recalling Pound's famous remark that poetry ought to be at least as well written as prose, Lee Mitchell proposes in *Mere Reading* that novels ought to be read at least as closely as poems; still dazzling in its fulfillment of this ambition is Ian Watt's "The First Paragraph of *The Ambassadors*." Once disruptive of poetic expectations, the now canonical prose-poem may be surveyed in David Lehman's English-language anthology, *Great American Prose Poems: From Poe to the Present*.

Poetry

In recent years, there has been among academic literary critics a renewed interest in the way we conceive of the lyric poem; Jonathan Culler's learned yet highly readable *Theory of the Lyric* feels like the culmination of this work. However revisionary, it stands on a body of venerable thinking about the lyric by Helen Vendler, Harold Bloom, R. P. Blackmur, and many others, not to mention the influential poet-critics, past and present, whose work I've already suggested.

Instructive as this work remains, there is of course no substitute for simply reading poems, which teach us how to read and write poems more efficiently than any work of criticism, including this one. If Wallace Stevens helps you to think about syntax, read Stevens. If Shakespeare helps you to think about figuration, read Shakespeare. "Nor is there singing school," said W. B. Yeats, "but studying / Monuments of its own magnificence."

BIBLIOGRAPHY

Adorno, Theodor. *Notes to Literature.* Translated by Shierry Weber Nicholsen. New York: Columbia University Press, 1991.

Arnold, Matthew. *The Poems.* Edited by Kenneth Allott. London: Longmans, 1965.

Ashbery, John. *Chinese Whispers.* New York: Farrar, Straus and Giroux, 2002.

———. *Where Shall I Wander.* New York: Ecco, 2005.

Aristotle. *Aristotle's Poetics.* Translated by S. H. Butcher. New York: Hill and Wang, 1966.

Attridge, Derek. *Poetic Rhythm: An Introduction.* Cambridge: Cambridge University Press, 1995.

Auden, W. H. *Collected Poems.* Edited by Edward Mendelson. New York: Random House, 1976.

Baker, William E. *Syntax in English Poetry 1870–1930.* Berkeley: University of California Press, 1967.

Barfield, Owen. *Poetic Diction: A Study in Meaning.* New York: McGraw-Hill, 1964.

Baugh, Albert, and Cable, Thomas. *A History of the English Language.* Fourth edition. Englewood Cliffs, NJ: Prentice Hall, 1993.

Bede. *Ecclesiastical History of the English People.* Edited by Bertram Colgrave and R.A.B. Mynors. New York: Oxford University Press, 1992.

Bernstein, Charles. *Content's Dream: Essays 1975–1984.* Los Angeles: Sun and Moon, 1986.

Bidart, Frank. *Half-Light: Collected Poems, 1965–2017.* New York: Farrar, Straus, and Giroux, 2017.

Bishop, Elizabeth. *Poems, Prose, and Letters.* Edited by Robert Giroux and Lloyd Schwartz. New York: Library of America, 2008.

Blake, William. *The Complete Poetry and Prose*. Edited by David Erdman. New York: Anchor Books, 1988.

Block, Ned. *Imagery*. Cambridge, Mass.: MIT Press, 1981.

Booth, Stephen. *An Essay on Shakespeare's Sonnets*. New Haven: Yale University Press, 1969.

Borges, Jorge Luis. *Labyrinths*. Edited by Donald Yates and James Irby. New York: New Directions, 1964.

Borroff, Marie. *Language and the Poet: Verbal Artistry in Frost, Stevens, and Moore*. Chicago: University of Chicago Press, 1979.

Brooke-Rose, Christine. *A Grammar of Metaphor*. London: Secker & Warburg, 1958.

Brooks, Cleanth, and Warren, Robert Penn. *Understanding Poetry*. New York: Henry Holt, 1938.

Browning, Robert. *A Critical Edition of the Major Works*. Edited by Adam Roberts. New York: Oxford University Press, 1997.

Burke, Kenneth. *Counter-Statement*. Berkeley: University of California Press, 1953.

Byron, George Gordon Lord. *Selected Poems*. Edited by Susan Wolfson and Peter Manning. New York: Penguin, 1996.

Caccini, Giulio. "Le nuove musiche." In *Source Readings in Music History*, edited by Oliver Strunk, pp. 377–92. New York: Norton, 1950.

Callimachus. *Hymns, Epigrams, Select Fragments*. Translated by Stanley Lombardo and Diane Rayor. Baltimore: Johns Hopkins University Press, 1988.

Campion, Thomas. *Songs from Rosseter's Book of Airs*. Edited by E. H. Fellowes. English School of Lutenist Song Writers, series 1, volume 13, part 2. London: Stainer and Bell, 1926.

———. *The Works of Thomas Campion*. Edited by Walter R. Davis. New York: Norton, 1970.

Cassidy, F. G., and Ringler, Richard. *Bright's Old English Grammar and Reader*. New York: Holt, 1971.

Chaucer, Geoffrey. *The Works of Geoffrey Chaucer*. Edited by F. N. Robinson. Boston: Houghton Mifflin, 1957.

Coleridge, Samuel Taylor. *Complete Poems*. Edited by William Keach. New York: Penguin, 1997.

———. *Table Talk*. Edited by Carl Woodring. 2 volumes. Princeton: Princeton University Press, 1990.

Crane, Hart. *Complete Poems and Selected Letters.* Edited by Langdon Hammer. New York: Library of America, 2006.

Culler, Jonathan. *Theory of the Lyric.* Cambridge, MA: Harvard University Press, 2015.

Davie, Donald. *Articulate Energy: An Inquiry into the Syntax of English Poetry.* London: Routledge, 1955.

———. *Purity of Diction in English Verse.* New York: Schocken, 1967.

Dickinson, Emily. *The Complete Poems.* Edited by Thomas H. Johnson. Boston: Little, Brown, 1960.

———. *The Letters.* Edited by Thomas H. Johnson. 3 volumes. Cambridge, MA: Harvard University Press, 1958.

———. *Poems: Third Series.* Edited by Mabel Loomis Todd. Boston: Roberts Brothers, 1896.

———. *The Poems: Variorum Edition.* Edited by R. W. Franklin. 3 volumes. Cambridge, MA: Harvard University Press, 1998.

Donne, John. *Collected Poetry.* Edited by Ilona Bell. New York: Penguin, 2012.

———. *Sermons on the Psalms and Gospels.* Edited by Evelyn Simpson. Berkeley: University of California Press, 1963.

Donoghue, Denis. *Metaphor.* Cambridge, MA: Harvard University Press, 2014.

Eliot, T. S. *Complete Poems and Plays.* New York: Harcourt, 1971.

———. "John Donne." *Nation and Athenaeum* 33 (9 June 1923): 331–32.

———. *Selected Essays.* New York: Harcourt, 1960.

Empson, William. *Argufying.* Edited by John Haffenden. Iowa City: University of Iowa Press, 1987.

———. *Seven Types of Ambiguity.* New York: New Directions, 1966.

Freud, Sigmund. "Remembering, Repeating, and Working Through." In *The Penguin Freud Reader,* edited by Adam Phillips, pp. 391–401. New York: Penguin, 2006.

Fries, Charles. *The Structure of English.* New York: Harcourt, 1952.

Frost, Robert. *Collected Poems, Prose, and Plays.* Edited by Richard Poirier and Mark Richardson. New York: Library of America, 1995.

Furbank, P. N. *Reflections on the Word "Image."* London: Secker & Warburg, 1970.

Gerber, Natalie. "Intonation and the Conventions of Free Verse." *Style* 49 (2015): 8–34.

Gogh, Vincent van. *Ever Yours: The Essential Letters*. Edited by Leo Jansen, Hans Luijten, and Nienke Bakker. New Haven: Yale University Press, 2014.

Greene, Roland, ed. *The Princeton Encyclopedia of Poetry and Poetics*. Fourth edition. Princeton: Princeton University Press, 2012.

Grossman, Allen. *The Long Schoolroom*. Ann Arbor: University of Michigan Press, 1997.

———. *The Sighted Singer: Two Works on Poetry for Readers and Writers*. Baltimore: Johns Hopkins University Press, 1992.

Hartman, Charles O. *Free Verse: An Essay on Prosody*. Princeton: Princeton University Press, 1980.

Hemingway, Ernest. *In Our Time*. New York: Scribner, 1958.

Hollander, John. *The Figure of Echo*. Berkeley: University of California Press, 1981.

———. *Melodious Guile: Fictive Patterns in Poetic Language*. New Haven: Yale University Press, 1988.

———. "Versions, Interpretations, and Performances." In *On Translation*, edited by Reuben Brower, pp. 205–31. Cambridge. MA: Harvard University Press, 1959.

Howe, Susan. *Souls of the Labadie Tract*. New York: New Directions, 2007.

James, Henry. *Literary Criticism*. Edited by Leon Edel. New York: Library of America, 1984.

Johnson, W. R. *The Idea of Lyric*. Berkeley: University of California Press, 1982.

Jonson, Ben. *The Complete Poems*. Edited George Parfitt. New York: Penguin, 1980.

Jorgens, Elise. *The Well-Tun'd Word: Musical Interpretations of English Poetry, 1597–1651*. Minneapolis: University of Minnesota Press, 1982.

Joyce, James. *Ulysses*. Edited by Hans Walter Gabler. New York: Random House, 1986.

Keats, John. *The Letters*. Edited by Hyder Edward Rollins. 2 volumes. Cambridge, MA: Harvard University Press, 1958.

———. *The Poems*. Edited by Jack Stillinger. London: Heinemann, 1978.

Kenner, Hugh. "Rhyme: An Unfinished Monograph." *Common Knowledge* 10 (2004): 377–425.

Kierkegaard, Søren. *Fear and Trembling and Repetition*. Edited and translated by Howard Hong and Edna Hong. Princeton: Princeton University Press, 1983.

Koethe, John. *The Constructor*. New York: HarperCollins, 1999.

Lakoff, George and Johnson, Mark. *Metaphors We Live By*. Chicago: University of Chicago Press, 1980.

Lanham, Richard. *A Handlist of Rhetorical Terms*. Berkeley: University of California Press, 1991.

Lawrence, D. H. *Complete Poems*. Edited by Vivian de Sola Pinto and Warren Roberts. New York: Penguin, 1964.

Leach, MacEdward. *The Ballad Book*. New York: Barnes, 1955.

Lehman, David. *Great American Prose Poems: From Poe to the Present*. New York: Scribner Poetry, 2003.

Lerer, Seth. *Inventing English*. New York: Columbia University Press, 2007.

Longenbach, James. *The Art of the Poetic Line*. Minneapolis: Graywolf Press, 2008.

Lowes, John Livingston. *The Road to Xanadu*. New York: Vintage, 1959.

Margulis, Elizabeth. *On Repeat: How Music Plays the Mind*. New York: Oxford University Press, 2014.

Milner, Marian. *On Not Being Able to Paint*. New York: International Universities Press, 1967.

Mitchell, Lee Clark. *Mere Reading: The Poetics of Wonder in Modern American Novels*. New York: Bloomsbury, 2017.

Mitchell, W.J.T. *Iconology: Image, Text, Ideology*. Chicago: University of Chicago Press, 1986.

Most, Glenn. "Greek Lyric Poets." In *Ancient Writers: Greece and Rome*, 2 volumes, edited by T. James Luce, vol. 1, pp. 75–98. New York: Scribner's, 1982.

Moore, Marianne. *Observations*. Edited by Linda Leavell. New York: Farrar, Straus and Giroux, 2015.

———. *Poems*. London: Egoist Press, 1921.

Opland, Jeff. *Anglo-Saxon Oral Poetry*. New Haven: Yale University Press, 1980.

Parkes, M. B. *Pause and Effect: An Introduction to the History of Punctuation in the West*. Berkeley: University of California Press, 1993.

Phillips, Adam. *Becoming Freud: The Making of a Psychoanalyst*. New Haven: Yale University Press, 2014.

Pinsky, Robert. *Gulf Music*. New York: Farrar, Straus and Giroux, 2007.

———. *The Sounds of Poetry*. New York: Farrar, Straus and Giroux, 1998.

Plato. *The Republic*. Translated by H.D.P. Lee. New York: Penguin, 1971.

Pound, Ezra. *ABC of Reading*. New York: New Directions, 1960.

———. *Gaudier-Brzeska*. New York: New Directions, 1970.

———. *Literary Essays*. Edited by T. S. Eliot. New York: New Directions, 1968.

———. *Personae*. Edited by Lea Baechler and A. Walton Litz. New York: New Directions, 1990.

Ransom, John Crowe. *The World's Body*. New York: Scribner's, 1938.

Richards, I. A. *Practical Criticism*. New York: Harcourt, 1929.

Ricks, Christopher. *The Force of Poetry*. New York: Oxford University Press, 1984.

Roe, Nicholas. *John Keats: A New Life*. New Haven: Yale University Press, 2012.

Scragg, Donald. "The Nature of Old English Verse." In *The Cambridge Companion to Old English Literature*, edited by Malcolm Godden and Michael Lapidge, pp. 55–70. Cambridge: Cambridge University Press, 1991.

Scarry, Elaine. *Dreaming by the Book*. New York: Farrar, Straus and Giroux, 1999.

Shakespeare, William. *Shakespeare's Sonnets*. Edited by Stephen Booth. New Haven: Yale University Press, 1977.

Smith, Barbara Herrnstein. *Poetic Closure: A Study of How Poems End*. Chicago: University of Chicago Press, 1968.

Stein, Gertrude. *Writings 1932–1946*. Edited by Catharine Stimpson and Harriet Chessman. New York: Library of America, 1998.

Stevens, Wallace. *Collected Poetry and Prose*. Edited by Frank Kermode and Joan Richardson. New York: Library of America, 1997.

Stewart, Susan. *Nonsense*. Baltimore: Johns Hopkins University Press, 1979.

———. *Poetry and the Fate of the Senses*. Chicago: University of Chicago Press, 2002.

———. *The Poet's Freedom: A Notebook on Making*. Chicago: University of Chicago Press, 2011.

Strand, Mark. *Collected Poems*. New York: Knopf, 2014.

Swinburne, Algernon Charles. *Selected Poetry and Prose*. Edited by John D. Rosenberg. New York: Modern Library, 1968.

Tench, Paul. *The Intonation Systems of English*. New York: Cassell, 1996.

Thompson. John. *The Founding of English Metre*. London: Routledge, 1961.

Toomer, Jean. *Cane*. New York: Liveright, 1975.

Voigt, Ellen Bryant. *The Art of Syntax*. Saint Paul: Graywolf Press, 2009.

———. *Headwaters*. New York: Norton, 2013.

———. *The Flexible Lyric*. Athens: University of Georgia Press, 1999.

Watt, Ian. "The First Paragraph of *The Ambassadors*: An Explication." *Essays in Criticism* 10 (1960): 250–74.

Williams, William Carlos. *The Collected Poems*. Edited by A. Walton Litz and Christopher MacGowan. 2 volumes. New York: New Directions, 1988.

Winn, James Anderson. *Unsuspected Eloquence: A History of the Relations between Poetry and Music*. New Haven: Yale University Press, 1981.

Wright, C. D. *Tremble*. New York: Ecco, 1996.

Wright, George T. "The Lyric Present: Simple Present Verbs in English Poems." *PMLA* 89 (1974): 563–79.

Wyatt, Sir Thomas. *The Complete Poems*. Edited by R. A. Rebholz. New Haven: Yale University Press, 1978.

———. *The Egerton Manuscript*. In *The Canon of Sir Thomas Wyatt's Poetry*, by Richard Harrier, pp. 95–254. Cambridge, MA: Harvard University Press, 1975.

Yeats, W. B. *The Poems*. Edited by Richard Finneran. New York: Scribner, 1997.

CREDITS

INDEX

Adorno, Theodore, 145
"America" (Bernstein and Sondheim), 115
"Among School Children" (Yeats), 146
Anacreon, 108, 131
"Andrea del Sarto" (Browning), 38
Aristotle, 49, 131
Arnold, Matthew, 122
Ashbery, John, 18, 36, 39
"As I Walked Out One Evening" (Auden), 86
"At Melville's Tomb" (Crane), 51–52, 150
"At the Fishhouses" (Bishop), 151–52
Auden, W. H., 86

"Bantams in Pine-Woods" (Stevens), 77
Bede, 142–44
"Below the surface-stream" (Arnold), 122
Bernstein, Leonard, 115
Bidart, Frank, 38–39, 121–22, 144–45
Bishop, Elizabeth, 151–52
"Black Jack Davey" (anonymous), 104–5, 113–14

Blake, William, 50–51, 52, 90, 92–93
Block, Ned, 85
Borges, Jorge Luis, 102
"Bright star, would I were steadfast as thou art" (Keats), 57
"Broken Heart, The" (Donne), 38
Brooks, Cleanth, 40
Browning, Robert, 38
Byron, George Gordon Lord, 65–68, 75, 77, 93, 150

Cædmon, 142–44, 145–46, 151
"Cædmon's Hymn," 143–44, 146, 147
Callimachus, 138
Campion, Thomas, 108–16
Cane (Toomer), 18, 134–36
"Canonization, The" (Donne), 33–35, 37, 43–44, 49, 80, 127–28, 150
Canterbury Tales, The (Chaucer), 17, 18, 21
"Celebration of Charis, A" (Jonson), 86–87
Chaucer, Geoffrey, 17, 18, 21
"Coin for Joe, with the Image of a Horse; c. 350–325 BC" (Bidart), 121

Coleridge, Samuel Taylor, 35, 146–49

"Constructor, The" (Koethe), 35–36

Crane, Hart, 51–52, 57, 58–59, 150

Dickinson, Emily, 29–31, 68–71, 75, 110–11, 122, 146

Donne, John, 33–35, 38–42, 44, 47, 49, 62, 76–77, 80, 88–89, 96, 127–28, 132, 150

Dowland, John, 108–9

Dylan, Bob, 104, 112

"Elevator" (Strand), 95, 96, 102–4, 110, 145

Eliot, T. S., 40–42, 88–89, 90

"Figure a Poem Makes, The" (Frost), 142

"Flame" (Wright), 87–89

Freud, Sigmund, 103, 151

Frost, Robert, 32, 33, 36, 66, 142

"Genesis 1–2:4" (Bidart), 144–45

"Georgia Dusk" (Toomer), 18

Giorgione, 15

Gogh, Vincent van, 83, 93

"Golden State" (Bidart), 39

"Good Morrow, The" (Donne), 38

"Grey Monk, The" (Blake), 50

"Gulf Music" (Pinsky), 78–80, 81

"Gypsy Laddie, The." *See* "Black Jack Davey"

Handy, W. C., 107

"Headwaters" (Voigt), 39

"He fumbles at your Soul" (Dickinson), 69–71, 75, 122, 146

Hemingway, Ernest, 132–34

"He Thinks of Those who have Spoken Evil of his Beloved" (Yeats), 145

Hollow Men, The (Eliot), 41

Homer, 136, 138

"Honky Tonk Woman" (Jagger and Richards), 107–8, 109

Horace, 138

Howe, Susan, 41, 90

"I Asked Mr. Dithers Whether It Was Time Yet He Said No to Wait" (Ashbery), 39

"In a Station of the Metro" (Pound), 63–65, 80, 84–95

In Our Time (Hemingway), 132–34

"Introduction to *The Tempest*" (James), 20–21

"Is it possible" (Wyatt), 97–98, 99, 102

"Is Your Town Nineveh?" (Moore), 38

"It may be good, like it who list" (Wyatt), 68

James, Henry, 20–21, 22, 101

"John Donne" (Eliot), 40

Johnson, Mark, 49

Johnson, Samuel, 42

Johnson, W. R., 131

Jonson, Ben, 86–87

Joyce, James, 18–19, 136–37

"Karintha" (Toomer), 134–36

Keats, John, 21, 53–59, 63, 123–24

Kierkegaard, Søren, 102, 140

Koethe, John, 35–36

"Kubla Khan" (Coleridge), 146–49

Lakoff, George, 49

Lawrence, D. H., 38, 44–46, 47

"Let me not to the marriage of true minds" (Shakespeare), 17, 18, 19, 62

Loews, John Livingston, 147

"Louie Louie" (Richard Berry), 74

"Love Song of J. Alfred Prufrock, The" (Eliot), 40–41, 90

Margulis, Elizabeth, 116

Milner, Marian, 19

Milton, John, 74

"Monkeys, The" (Moore). *See* "My Apish Cousins"

Monroe, Harriet, 51, 52

Moore, Marianne, 22–25, 38, 80, 98–101, 110, 149

Most, Glenn, 108

"My Apish Cousins" (Moore), 22–25, 80, 98–99, 101, 149

"My life closed twice before its close" (Dickinson), 110–11

"My sweetest Lesbia, let us live and love" (Campion), 138

"Nephelidia" (Swinburne), 77

"New York" (Moore), 100–101

"No Possum, No Sop, No Taters" (Stevens), 29–33, 133

"Not Ideas about the Thing but the Thing Itself" (Stevens), 81

Observations (Moore), 101

"Observations on the Art of English Poesie" (Campion), 109

"Ode to a Nightingale" (Keats), 56–57

Odyssey (Homer), 136

"Of Mere Being" (Stevens), 80

"On First Looking into Chapman's Homer" (Keats), 21

"On Tone" (Voigt), 128–29

Paradise Lost (Milton), 74

Phillips, Adam, 56–57

Picasso, Pablo, 20

"Pierre Menard, Author of the Quixote" (Borges), 102

Pindar, 131

Pinsky, Robert, 78–80, 81

Plato, 107, 108, 131

Professor Longhair (Henry Roeland Byrd), 78–79

"Pomegranate" (Lawrence), 38, 44–46

Pope, Alexander, 42

Pound, Ezra, 63–65, 67, 68, 80, 84–85, 88, 93, 108

"Prologue to the Aetia" (Callimachus), 138

Propertius, 138

"Queen-Anne's-Lace" (Williams), 86

Ransom, John Crowe, 52–53, 56, 62

Rauschenberg, Robert, 15

"Relic, The" (Donne), 88, 89

"Retrospect, A" (Pound), 84

Richards, I. A., 119

Rolling Stones, The, 107–8, 109

"St. Louis Blues" (Handy), 107

Sappho, 61, 108, 131

"Seafarer, The" (anonymous), 16–17, 21, 23, 61

Seeger, Pete, 104

"Sermon Preached at the Funerals of Sir William Cokayne Knight" (Donne), 76–77, 96

Shakespeare, William, 17, 18, 19, 20–21, 36, 38, 52–54, 56, 57, 59, 62, 63, 73, 77, 80, 81, 88–89, 96, 110, 111, 122–23, 138, 146, 150

"Sleep" (Voigt), 46–47, 68, 126–29, 134

"Somnambulisma" (Stevens), 124

Sonnets (Shakespeare), 17, 18, 19, 52–54, 56, 57, 59, 62, 73, 77, 80, 81, 88, 96, 111, 122–23, 146, 150

"Souls of the Labadie Tract" (Howe), 90

"So, we'll go no more a roving" (Byron), 65–67, 75, 77, 93, 150

Stein, Gertrude, 102

Stevens, Wallace, 29–33, 63, 77–78, 80–81, 133, 138

"Stopping by Woods on a Snowy Evening" (Frost), 32, 33, 36

Strand, Mark, 95–96, 102–4, 110, 145

Swinburne, Algernon Charles, 77

Tennyson, Alfred Lord

"Tipitina" (Professor Longhair), 78–79

"To a Poor Old Woman" (Williams), 124–26

"To Autumn" (Keats), 123–24

Toomer, Jean, 18, 134–36

"To Shakespeare" (Crane), 58–59

"Tower, The" (Yeats), 24–25, 35

Ulysses (Joyce), 18–19, 136–37

Voigt, Ellen Bryant, 39, 46–47, 68, 126–29, 134

"Vorticism" (Pound), 84–85

Warren, Robert Penn, 40

Waste Land, The (Eliot), 40–41

"Western Wind" (anonymous), 27–29, 33, 36, 110, 133

West Side Story (Bernstein and Sondheim), 115

"When I do count the clock that tells the time" (Shakespeare), 53–54, 80, 81, 88, 96, 122–23, 146, 150

"When thou must home to shades of under ground" (Campion), 111, 114

"Where Shall I Wander" (Ashbery), 18

"Why is my verse so barren of new pride" (Shakespeare), 36

Williams, William Carlos, 86, 93, 124–26, 128

Wright, C. D., 87–89, 93

Wyatt, Sir Thomas, 68, 97–98, 99, 102, 135

Yeats, W. B., 24–25, 145, 146

Zukofsky, Louis, 41